HARDCORE

by **Jonathan Hall**

Cast

Craig	Luke Evans
Kevin	Simon Thomas
Robert	Christopher Redmond
Martin	Phil Matthews

First performed at Pleasance Theatre on 29 June 2004

HARDCORE
by **Jonathan Hall**

Director	Russell Labey
Designer	Jason Denvir
Lighting Designer	Richard House
Music	Leon Parris
Stage Manager	Naomi Lee
General Manager	Guy Chapman and Kate Graham-Campbell for Guy Chapman Associates Assisted by Sophie Curtis
Marketing	Mathew Smith for Guy Chapman Associates
Press	Kevin Wilson for KWPR (020 7430 2060)
Graphic design	Andrew Newsom Design
Photography	Robert Workman

With thanks to: Rio Beach (Earlham Street), Fenchurch, Derek Walters, Ben Buckby-Jones, Mike Ross, Nick Quinn at The Agency, Ollie Rance, Christopher Richardson, Paul Cullen, *Spotlight*, Vertec Printing Services, Guido Goetz, St Gabriels Rehearsal Rooms.

PLEASANCE
THEATRE • ISLINGTON
www.pleasance.co.uk

For the Pleasance Theatre

Director	Christopher Richardson
Deputy Director	Anthony Alderson
Business Manager	Jose Ferran
London Programmers	Ollie Rance & Claire Nightingale
Stage Manager	Ryan Taylor
Marketing Assistant	Beci Ryan
Deputy Marketing Assistant	Tim Standing
Master Carpenter	Will Jackson
Accounts	Yvonne Goddard
Web Designer	Stephane Levy
Cleaner	Maria Meme

For Pleasance Theatre Festival, Edinburgh

Production Manager	Mandy Castile
Programme Co-ordinators	Claire Nightingale and Ollie Rance

Associate Directors, Young Pleasance Kathryn Norton, Tim Norton

The settings are built by Will Jackson in the Pleasance Theatre Workshops.

Pleasance Theatre Festival Ltd is a company registered in England and Wales and is a wholly owned subsidiary of the Pleasance Theatre Trust, a registered charity no 1050944

Cast

Luke Evans Craig

Luke is 25 and is from South Wales.
Theatre credits include: Theo in the original London cast of *La Cava* (2000-01), Billy in the original London cast of *Taboo* (2002) and Chris in the UK Tour of *Miss Saigon* (2003).
TV Credits include: Sean from *Crossroads* (2002).
Albums: *La Cava* London Cast recording and *Taboo* London Cast recording.
Luke is very pleased to be joining the Cast of *Hardcore*.

Simon Thomas Kevin

Training: Guildford School of Acting
Theatre includes: The Prince in Roger and Hammerstein's musical *Cinderella* at the Bristol Old Vic, Will in *Only the Brave* at the New Theatre in Cardiff, Kevin in *Hardcore* at the Pleasance Edinburgh, The Nuffield Theatre's tour of *Rattle of A Simple Man* understudying the role of Richard, Bob Fry in *The Dreaming* at The Yvonne Arnaud Theatre and Edinburgh Festival, Stingo in the *Kissing Dance* (UK tour), The Barman in Richard Stilgoe's *Exit Allan* at the Sherman Theatre in Cardiff, Lewis in *Pippin* at the Electric Theatre Guildford, Sam in *The Ragged Child* at The Danny and Sylvia Kaye Playhouse, New York.
Concerts include: Andrew Lloyd Webber's Fiftieth Birthday Celebration at the Royal Albert Hall.
Recordings include: Will in *Only the Brave*, Bob Fry in *The Dreaming*, Balthazar in *The Rock Nativity*.

Christopher Redmond Robert

Since graduating from the Welsh College of Music in 2002, Chris has appeared as Aladdin in *Aladdin – The Wok and Roll Panto* and Billy Goose in *Mother Goose* both at the Liverpool Everyman. He was also in *The Handmaid's Tale* at the English National Opera.

Phil Matthews Martin

Graduated from The Central School of Speech and Drama in London where he won the 2002 Sir John Gielgud Bursary Award and finished the course with Distinction.
Theatre includes: Shelley in Liz Lochhead's *Blood and Ice* at the Royal Lyceum, Edinburgh, Martin in *Hardcore*, Edinburgh. Michael in *Get out of that then!* (Live Theatre), Nicky in *The Young Ones* (New Tyne Theatre), Jack in *Acting Out* (Drill Hall).
Television credits include: Gabriel Roystan in *Catherine Cookson's 'A Dinner of Herbs'* (ITV), Phil in *Blind Ambition* (ITV), Raoul in *The Gift* (BBC), Dean Sinton in *Byker Grove* (BBC), Sigfrith in *Zig Zag Invaders* (BBC). Radio: *Go For It* (BBC Radio 4).

Production Team

Jonathan Hall Writer

Jonathan Hall is twice winner of The Edinburgh Festival Fringe First Award for *Sweet As You Are* and *Behind the Aquarium at the Last Pizza Show*. Other awards include D H Lawrence Short Story Competition Award and The Joshua Tetley Drama Award. He's written for television, radio and theatre and past work includes: *Nativity* (Bradford and Edinburgh), *Enthusiastic Men* (Bradford and Edinburgh), *Statements of Attainment* (Bradford and Edinburgh), *Buy* (Bradford and Edinburgh), *Beowulf* (Bradford and Edinburgh *Behind the Aquarium at the Last Pizza Show* (Bradford, Edinburgh and Chester), *Beauty and the Beast* (Chester), *Wind in the Willows* (Bradford), *Rollover Dreaming* (Bradford), *Sweet As You Are* (Y Touring, Edinburgh And London), *Learning to Love the Grey* (Y Touring. Edinburgh and UK tour), *Over the Edge of the World* (HM Prison Wayland), *Charley's Aunt* (BBC Radio 4), *Flamingos* (Bush Theatre, Director Mike Bradwell), *Learning to Love the Grey*, *Making Astronauts* (Original Television Plays For The BBC), *Forty Nine and Up For It*, (Play for BBC Choice), *The Nature of Vikings* (BBC Radio 4), *The Best Bit* (Nottingham Playhouse/ Northampton Theatre), *The Coffee Lovers' Guide to America* (Chelsea Theatre), *Mr Elliott* (Chelsea Theatre), *Hardcore* (Edinburgh Fringe).

Hardcore and *Plays* collection of Jonathan's works are both published by Oberon Books.

Russell Labey Director

Theatre: As Director/Writer: *New Boy* (New York, London, Edinburgh, UK Tour), *Whistle Down the Wind* (Sadler's Wells, Riverside Studios, London, Edinburgh Festival Theatre, West Yorkshire Playhouse and extensive UK Tour). As Director: *Hardcore* (Edinburgh), *Bugsy Malone* (Queens Theatre, West End), *The Dreaming* and *The Kissing Dance*, both by Charles Hart and Howard Goodall (Linbury Theatre, Royal Opera House, Covent Garden and UK Tour) and *Drake*, *Joseph And The Amazing Technicolor Dreamcoat*, *Once Upon a War* and *Tin Pan Ali*, all for the NYMT. As Resident Director: *Sunset Boulevard* (Really Useful Group, UK Tour).

Russell has been commissioned to write and direct a new play for the Theatre Royal, Plymouth and is working on the screenplay of *New Boy*. Television: As Presenter: *Inside Out* (BBC), *Spotlight* (BBC), *Collectors' Lot* (Channel 4), *The Windors*, *Sale of a Lifetime* (Channel 4).

Jason Denvir Designer

Has worked in UK, Japan, Singapore, and New York.
Jason designed *New Boy* for the same production company. Other Design Work includes; *Mother Goose*, *A Song at Twilight*, *Carousel*, *Cinderella*, *Annie*, *Oklahoma!*, *Mistress of the Inn*, and *The Innocents*; all for Perth Theatre. *Beyond The Door*; for Simane Regional Development Foundation, Huko Topia, Tokyo, Japan. *Into The Woods*, *The Threepenny Opera*, *Tin*

Pan Ali, *Guys and Dolls*, *Oliver!*; for Nation Music Theatre Company.
Barber of Seville; for European Chamber Opera. *Robin Hood*; for Polka
Theatre. He has worked in production at RADA, and The Queens Theatre,
Barnstaple. Jason also lectures in design at RADA and Middlesex University,
and at City Literary Institute.

Richard House Lighting Designer

Has worked with a wide range of artists from English National Ballet to
Rowan Atkinson and also specialises in large outdoor events at venues
such as Blenheim Palace. He has worked extensively for the NYMT: shows
include *Captain Stirrick, Jack Spratt VC, Joseph, Bodywork, The Little
Rats, Once Upon a War and The Ragged Child* and *Pendragon*. Richard lit
New Boy and *Whistle Down the Wind* on their successful UK dates and
Bugsy Malone on its UK tour and in the West End. Advancing into middle
age, Richard's focus is now more on his roles as trustee of the charitable
trust running the flourishing Pleasance Theatres in Edinburgh and London,
and as trustee of the Kingston Theatre, currently being built, which will
have Sir Peter Hall as its Artistic Director.

Leon Parris Composer

Began his career at the National Youth Music Theatre working on the
original *Whistle Down the Wind* which toured to the Edinburgh Festival
and then came in to Sadler's Wells. Subsequently he was Assistant Musical
Arranger for *Bugsy Malone* at The Queens Theatre London. Leon is a
Qualified Vocal Coach and trained at the National Music Theatre.
Between 2000 and 2002 Leon worked with Hat Trick productions on the
music and soundscape for a variety of television and advertising projects.
During 2001 he worked with Brian Clemens (creator of *The Professionals*,
The Avengers et al) on a number of projects writing music and working on
sound design for television and film. The following year saw him compose
the music and design the soundscape for the sci-fi trilogy *Earthsearch:
Mindwarp* by James Follett for Big Finish Productions, which was published
in 2003.
At present Leon is working on the sound design and score for a series of
short films for the Edinburgh Film Festival.
Awards and Bursaries: The Really Useful Group Award for Most Promising
Young Writer, The Warner Chappell Award, The Mercury Workshops Award
(Cameron Macintosh) and The Vivian Ellis Award for Best Musical. In
2001 Leon was given a Cameron Macintosh Bursary.

Naomi Lee Stage Manager

Naomi graduated from the technical and stage management course at
Mountview Academy of Theatre Arts in July 2001. In the first year of her
career she worked on a wide variety of fringe and small scale productions
before spending 18 months touring the UK as ASM/book cover with *Buddy*.
Naomi has spent the last nine months as ASM swing on *Thoroughly Modern
Millie* at the Shaftesbury Theatre.

HARDCORE

First published in 2004 by Oberon Books Ltd
(incorporating Absolute Classics)
521 Caledonian Road, London N7 9RH
Tel: 020 7607 3637 / Fax: 020 7607 3629
e-mail: oberon.books@btinternet.com
www.oberonbooks.com

A catalogue record for this book is available from the British
Library.

ISBN: 1 84002 493 3

Printed in Great Britain by Antony Rowe Ltd, Chippenham.

Characters

CRAIG, twenty-three

MARTIN, twenty-two

ROBERT, twenty-six

KEVIN, twenty-six

The characters play other people as specified by the text.

A note on the staging
The scenes should flow into each other in a smooth and snappy, almost 'filmic' way; the joins marked by sound and light and movement. In light of this it is therefore best to keep the setting as minimal and abstract as possible.

To Simon

HARDCORE

Scene One

The noise of the sea. CRAIG steps forward into a spotlight. Early twenties, young but with a certain hard veneer about him.

CRAIG: Well I suppose for me sex is about excitement – energy – the best for me is somewhere anonymous – somewhere like a dark room in a club. Someone looks, they look away. You look back, they look back. They follow you… And all the time the music's going on and there's the smell of poppers and sweat – you're pushing your way through the bodies – them following you – and then you're both there in the dark – it's good. Just you and them. And then afterwards – no complications. No shit.

A question is asked to which he responds.

I was a student – fuck-all money, loads of debts – so I did a bit of modelling – just some photo shoots – not brilliantly paid – but better than serving in some bar somewhere. Anyway, one of the producers from this video company saw my shots – contacted me – suggested I did a screen test – which led to my doing my first film, *Release of Tension* – (*Smiles.*) Thank you. Yes I was having a good time. (*His smile becomes more suggestive.*)

ROBERT and KEVIN step from each side and stand to the side and back of CRAIG. CRAIG is now flirting big time.

Well – without wanting to sound big headed I'd say I was good at having sex in front of a camera – and if you're good at doing something – you enjoy doing it – and I guess that shows. I suppose it arouses me to arouse others.

Music up as ROBERT and KEVIN step forward, looking hesitant and nervous.

KEVIN: All the way?

ROBERT: Stop at pants –

KEVIN: – right you are –

ROBERT: I gave you the Polaroids earlier?

The two start to strip. They're much less practised than CRAIG.

CRAIG: Since I've been in this business I suppose I've got a bit spoilt – I realise that sex is only really good with guys who know what they're doing. Know what they're doing and are good at it. Well – other performers. Other porn actors, couple of escorts. A Chippendale. Why go back to the valley when you've climbed the mountain peaks? (*His hand drops to his cock.*)

ROBERT: Why do I want to be in a porno film? Gosh. (*Laughs.*) Can I phone a friend? Basically I suppose it's something that's always appealed. Something on 'the wish list' if you like. That and paragliding –

KEVIN: I'm an actor –

ROBERT: I'm 27 next month. Time's passing by, you gotta do these things –

KEVIN: Things have been really quiet – I mean really – you ask anyone – you can't catch a cold at the moment. So I've done some extra work, *The Bill, EastEnders,* ya di ya di ya – and me and a mate, we're putting together this comedy tape – which I'm really excited about – but I came to the conclusion that what I *really* need to do was give the career a bit of a kickstart as it were – (*Agreeing with comment.*) By being in a porn film. No – actually I'm straight as a matter of fact –

ROBERT: My partner? He's all for it.

KEVIN: You see I see being in 'a gay adult motion picture', unquote, as a way of demonstrating my versatility – I mean a straight bloke in a gay film – what could be more versatile than that?

ROBERT: Sex with others? I suppose that'd all depend on the others –

KEVIN: Sex with men? (*Shrugs.*) It's all acting. Hey, I worked as a hospital porter once – I'm not easily shocked. (*CRAIG steps forward.*)

CRAIG: Rimming – sucking – fucking – threesomes – all the usual. (*Responding to a comment.*) Certainly. (*His hand begins to work his dick more frantically.*)

KEVIN: What arouses me?

ROBERT: Now you're asking –

KEVIN: It's got to be touch – mutual touching – lots of kissing – to start things off –

ROBERT: Older men –

KEVIN: This is all with a woman of course –

ROBERT: Definitely older men –

KEVIN: Spontaneity – that's got to be a big part of it.

ROBERT: Hairy chests –

KEVIN: Lots of mutual 'caressment' – is that a word?

ROBERT: You see my partner's a bit older than me. Fifty-two. Sorry, no, I don't know why I'm smiling –

KEVIN: The mood has to be right.

In the background we hear the sound of CRAIG coming.

ROBERT: I have these fantasies – older men mostly – Daddies…pupil-teacher-tastic…you know the sort of thing.

KEVIN: Jess, my girlfriend – she has these aromatherapy oils she rubs into my feet which I tell you is just amazing. A man? Well (*Ticking off on his fingers.*) hugging – no problem, fondling – no problem – blow job – well, I wouldn't mind him doing it to me – provided I could get it up as t'were. Anything else – we might be talking a bit of a problem. (*They fade into the background leaving just CRAIG.*)

CRAIG: (*Cleaning himself up.*) It's not an emotional thing at all – why should it be? Just someone you meet – Have sex – move on. No complications. Like life should be.

The music rises to a climax and then abruptly cuts out to reveal ROBERT sat in his underpants. KEVIN enters in his underwear texting into a mobile phone. They catch sight of each other and smile sheepishly. ROBERT puts his jacket on.

KEVIN: You've got the right idea –

ROBERT: Yes –

KEVIN: It is a bit of the old brass monkeys in here – (*He puts his jacket on.*)

ROBERT: It is rather –

KEVIN: Fellow auditionee I presume –

ROBERT: Certainly am –

KEVIN: Kevin –

KEVIN puts his hand out to shake – as does ROBERT. They both remember what they've been doing and retract them hastily.

ROBERT: Robert – (*Embarrassed.*) Bit of a dive – I take it you're waiting for the photos –

KEVIN: Yes – yes I am –

ROBERT: I wonder how much longer they're going to be –

KEVIN: These things always take time –

ROBERT: You've done them before?

KEVIN: No – at least not these sorts of photos – (*Pause.*) So what is it you do then Robert?

ROBERT: I work in finance –

KEVIN: Ah –

ROBERT: Yourself?

KEVIN: Actor –

ROBERT: An act*or* my goodness – a real actor?

KEVIN: Sorry?

ROBERT: I mean –

KEVIN: God yes – no, this is all new to me, all this – I'm kickstarting the career – as it were –

ROBERT: So what have you been in before now?

KEVIN: How long have you got? No seriously, the last thing I did was *EastEnders* –

ROBERT: Oh? Playing?

KEVIN: Man in the market. The last *theatre* thing I did was up at the Abattoir –

ROBERT: The where?

KEVIN: Fringe place in Camden? Cutting edge for new writing – I did a piece about child abuse – *Dolly Mixtures* –

ROBERT: Right –

KEVIN: Cutting edge –

ROBERT: Right – (*Pause.*)

KEVIN: Bloody cold.

ROBERT: You think they'd have some heating of some description.

KEVIN: Yeah – (*A pause.*)

ROBERT: Where have you come from then?

KEVIN: Pinner –

ROBERT: Oh right. Which way did you come?

KEVIN: North circular –

ROBERT: What's that like on a weekend?

KEVIN: A nightmare – road works near Swiss Cottage – but it's never *good.*

ROBERT: There's this cut-through I use –

KEVIN: Oh?

ROBERT: Up Hampstead Heath –

KEVIN: Any good?

ROBERT: Speed bump city but loads quicker.

CRAIG walks on, still in his underwear. Instantly they're both awkward again.

CRAIG: All right?

ROBERT: Ah – another auditionee –

CRAIG: How's it going?

KEVIN: All right mate – good. Kevin –

ROBERT: Robert.

CRAIG: Craig – they said five minutes for the photos – (*Obviously pissed off.*) They're just getting the lights set up – though how they expect to get any decent shots with those lights is beyond me –

ROBERT: So does anyone know what these photos are? I mean apart from the obvious –

CRAIG: They just want some shots of us together – so they

can see how we look. It's what they do in auditions like these – even a half-arsed set-up like this –

ROBERT: You seem to know what you're talking about –

CRAIG: I do –

KEVIN: You've done this sort of thing before? (*CRAIG nods.*)

CRAIG: I have –

ROBERT: Films? (*CRAIG nods.*) How many?

CRAIG: Two. *Release of Tension* – and one of the 'Bad Brit Boys' series –

ROBERT: Quite the old hand –

CRAIG: Bit of a better set-up I tell you. (*Looks around.*) Studio.

KEVIN: They said their main one was in use.

CRAIG: So the Brownies meet on Saturdays now, do they? Mind you it's what you expect. It's a joke over here –

ROBERT: What is?

CRAIG: Porn. One step up from home movies. I mean you should see the set up in Europe – or the States. Especially the States. So – have either of you done work like this before?

ROBERT: First timer me.

CRAIG: Kevin?

KEVIN: I'm not likely to have – (*CRAIG looks questioningly at him.*) I bat for the other side see – I'm straight.

CRAIG: Straight.

KEVIN: I'm an actor see – wanting to give the old career a bit of a kick-start. Show my versatility. And what could be more versatile than a straight guy in a gay film?

CRAIG: Right. (*To ROBERT.*) So are you straight as well?

ROBERT: No – just bored. I didn't say that.

CRAIG: Two novices –

ROBERT: And an old hand –

CRAIG: (*Getting out hip flask.*) Well here's to you. Best of luck –

MARTIN bursts in.

MARTIN: This *is* the place where make the porno films – (*He clocks the others.*) Silly question Martin. I'm not too late am I? The tube was just crazy – I'm like stood there on the platform shouting 'I'm late for an audition for a porn film' – I could see them looking at me thinking 'Hello, we have a weirdo in our midst' –

ROBERT: They're just through there.

MARTIN: So you're all the act*ors* right? Sorry – I mean you're all performers in the 'adult erotica'.

ROBERT: We don't know –

KEVIN: We're waiting to hear.

ROBERT: Do we pass muster –

KEVIN: Craig is, though – he's been in two –

MARTIN: I'll ask for your autograph now. (*By now CRAIG has written him off as a tosser and has retreated.*) So it's okay in there? Les auditions?

KEVIN: It's fine mate.

ROBERT: They didn't eat me anyway –

MARTIN: They don't want me to read Shakespeare or anything terribly intellectual like that?

KEVIN: I thought that – I learnt this whole speech from *Shopping and Fucking* – it's a play –

MARTIN: Only I'm telling you now if they do 'Martin has left the building'.

ROBERT: It's fine –

MARTIN: So what do they want you to do? (*CRAIG and ROBERT look embarrassed.*)

ROBERT: Just talk a bit about yourself really –

KEVIN: A bit of the old life story –

MARTIN: Are they ready for this I ask myself.

CRAIG: And wank yourself off of course –

MARTIN: Hey I'd rather do that than read Shakespeare – (*Exits.*)

Cut to the audition room.

MARTIN: Martin – oh sorry – of course. (*Sits on stool.*) That better? Martin – Martin Thomas.

I don't know – I might've seen one or two – *Overload?* – like I say, I don't know. One doesn't usually watch the credits – one usually fast forwards to a good bit, has, shall we say, a nice time and then one switches it off –

Has Martin got a boyfriend now? I think the answer to that one is 'watch this space'.

ROBERT and CRAIG are stood in their underwear waiting for the photo session.

ROBERT: This is taking forever.

CRAIG: They have to make sure the light's right.

ROBERT: I see. So these *Overload* films – are they any good?

CRAIG: Have you seen any?

ROBERT: I don't think so –

CRAIG: The critics seem to think so.

ROBERT: Oh?

CRAIG: *Release of Tension* was nominated for three Stiffies last year –

ROBERT: (*Laughing.*) What-ies?

CRAIG: Gay erotic Oscars –

ROBERT: One of the guys was saying – didn't you win some award?

CRAIG: Most promising newcomer.

ROBERT: Very impressive.

CRAIG: Thank you.

ROBERT: So are you able to live the life of a wealthy porn star?

CRAIG: On what this pays? I wish.

ROBERT: Is it not well paid?

CRAIG: Two fifty to three a scene. It's a joke. You'll be lucky to get away with seven or eight.

ROBERT: I always thought it was pretty lucrative.

CRAIG: That's the States –

ROBERT: The land of plenty –

CRAIG: Too right – hello, this is us –

ROBERT: Right.

CRAIG: Don't worry too much – they're just pairing shots – (*Flash.*)

ROBERT: So what else do you do then? When you're not modelling?

CRAIG: Sell a bit of E. Bit of escort work. Temping if I'm really hard up.

ROBERT: Temping? In offices?

CRAIG: Very dull and boring and shite.

ROBERT: What isn't?

CRAIG: What about you?

ROBERT: Finance.

CRAIG: Oh?

ROBERT: I sell Lifestyle plans to incredibly rich gay men.

CRAIG: Is this in the city?

ROBERT: For my sins.

CRAIG: Well paid?

ROBERT: Not as much as I'd like. Forty-five a year.
   Bonuses on top of that.

CRAIG: So what if one of your clients sees you on film?

ROBERT: Knowing my clients it'll do me no end of good.
   (*Steps in something.*) God, this place is rancid.

Cut back to the audition room.

MARTIN: Martin Thomas is a creation. Basically I was
   eighteen, in a crappy job in a old folks' home, all had
   gone pear-shaped with the love of my life – well, I
   looked at myself and thought life was going to be a
   whole lot better if I became someone else. So I moved
   down to London, got some work doing various bits and
   pieces – and discovered the scene in one helluva big
   way. And all the people who slagged me off and put me
   down – well, they're still in the same job they were in
   after leaving school having failed their GCSEs –

   The love of my life? Well it didn't work out. What was
   the problem? His wife wasn't too keen, that was one
   fairly major stumbling block.

Okay – down to the bare? Right you are – pants on – my pulling pants, I hope you're duly impressed. (*He strips, rather clumsily and endearingly.*) God, I'm sorry, I'm really bad at this. I'm better if there's a gorgeous six-foot black guy sat on the bed wearing nothing but an inviting expression.

How would I feel about sleeping with someone I didn't fancy? Think of the money – (*He smiles cheekily.*)

Cut to the changing room. KEVIN and CRAIG are similarly posing for the cameras.

KEVIN: This okay? Right.

CRAIG: So are you really straight then?

KEVIN: Ring my girlfriend, she'll tell you. Why, is that a problem?

CRAIG: You've never been with a man?

KEVIN: *Cage aux Folles* at Worcester Civic – that's as close as it's got.

CRAIG: To date. (*Flash.*)

KEVIN: God, it's bloody cold – So come on then – one actor to another – what's it like then?

CRAIG: What's what like?

KEVIN: Gay sex.

CRAIG: Depends?

KEVIN: On?

CRAIG: If you like sex with a man. If you don't then pretty crap I should say.

KEVIN: Is it like sex with a woman?

CRAIG: I wouldn't know.

KEVIN: You'd be surprised how many straight men are curious about it –

CRAIG: You'll be able to enlighten them won't you.

KEVIN: I have to ask – do you ever have any trouble?

CRAIG: Trouble?

KEVIN: Well – standing to attention as it were –

CRAIG: It's known as 'getting wood'. And no.

KEVIN: I just wondered – sometimes – under the camera –

CRAIG: Don't worry about it – there's always Saint Viagra – (*Flash. They exit.*)

Cut back to MARTIN's audition.

MARTIN: Why do I want to be in a 'gay adult motion picture'? To make me famous? To make me infamous more like – I mean you dream – everyone does – I mean one never knows what it might lead to. (*Deep voice.*) 'Martin – you have entered the *Big Brother* house' –

(*Normal voice.*) And say 'Mr Right' *is* out there – he's not going to see me shut away in my little bedsit now is he?

The scene cuts to the pub round the corner. Christmas music plays. The noise of people talking. KEVIN and ROBERT are sat there looking a little uncomfortable. ROBERT is texting.

KEVIN: It'll be like when I was in a Mountain Rescue team for *Emergency 999*.

ROBERT: Sorry?

CRAIG comes on talking into his phone.

KEVIN: I don't know one end of a crampon from another – but you learn. That's acting.

CRAIG: So the Yard about ten – okay – right – (*Switches off phone.*)

ROBERT: (*Looking at the phone.*) Nice –

CRAIG: It needs upgrading –

ROBERT: Pictures?

CRAIG: Of course – cheers.

ROBERT: The Yard –

CRAIG: Just to start with.

ROBERT: I've heard it's good there.

CRAIG: It's gone off a bit lately. But it's only to start with – So, good day everyone?

ROBERT: Different.

CRAIG: Not put off?

KEVIN: Like I was saying – it's just a job –

MARTIN enters.

MARTIN: That man over there is so cute –

ROBERT: Which one –

MARTIN: The one in the leather jacket. (*Sits.*) Would you just listen to me – I mean here's this guy eyeing me up and here I am auditioning for a part in a porn film. This is sad; this is very sad – Anyway lads – (*The others respond.*) Here's to us budding porno stars.

The others look round embarrassed. MARTIN is unaware – he holds a hand up as a Rosemary Clooney singing 'Have Yourself a Merry Little Christmas' comes on.

Guilty –

ROBERT: Into the slushy songs are you?

MARTIN: Only in a cynical bitter and twisted fuck off you bastard sort of way.

KEVIN: So how did you get on then Martin?

MARTIN: What?

ROBERT: Your audition.

MARTIN: I don't know why I was getting so worked up – I mean one look at those other guys and without being big headed I basically knew I had absolutely nothing to worry about in the looks department –

CRAIG: There's a little bit more to it than that –

MARTIN: Anyway, I did the business – gave them the old life history, rattled on a bit – got my todger out – and then they asked me what was my most arousing moment –

ROBERT: They asked me that –

KEVIN: And me –

CRAIG: They ask everyone that.

MARTIN: Well my mind went completely blank – and I thought – hey – is it possible I've got to the ripe old age of twenty-two without ever having an arousing moment, – but then I remembered Mr Fly-Mo.

ROBERT: Who?

MARTIN: Next door neighbour – the lurve of mah life –

ROBERT: Mr Fly-Mo?

MARTIN: He had one – along with a wife, two kids and a timeshare in Normandy. I know: the love of my life had a fly-mo, how sad is that we ask ourselves.

KEVIN: So what happened with this – Mr Fly-Mo?

MARTIN: Well – are you sitting comfortably? Martin's most arousing moment. This all happened when I was sixteen – about the time I started thinking 'Hey Martin, maybe you're more into boys than you are into girls' – Anyway our neighbour used to do the garden a lot –

regular Alan Titchmarsh he was – used to wear just these skimpy cut off denims – brilliant body, really fit – we are talking serious attractiveness here.

Anyway – it was summer – absolutely baking – so he was out in the garden more than usual – and I was getting ready to fail my A-levels in a spectacular way so I was up in the bedroom revising – though truth be told I spent more time ogling down at his Lordship doing his *Groundforce* bit. Occasionally he'd see me – look up, smile – wave –

Anyhow, one day I was working away when I see his fly-mo's packed up. So down I toddles to see if I can help as you do. Well it was simple enough – a case of a disconnected lead – three minutes and we were back in business. Anyway Martin's definitely man of the moment after this so to cut a short story long he produces a couple of cans of Woodpecker Cider. And we sit out on the patio in the sun. And he's sat there in his skimpy shorts – legs up on the patio wall – I had this massively erotic view of his electric blue bikini briefs. Anyway by now what with the drink and him sat there I was getting quite erectomondo, when suddenly he says, 'I don't know about you but I could do with a shower' – up he springs and goes inside. I follow him in, talk about a stiffy. I could've pole-vaulted up those stairs. So I go in, I strip off and showers, expecting all the time for him to come in – but no sign of him. Eventually I gets dressed and I hear this other shower – off their bedroom, en suite jobby. Avocado. So shaking all over I summon up my courage and in – and there he is showering. When he sees me he steps out, stark naked. All the hair on his body going one way with the water. Smell of Brut shower gel. I said 'Oh, I'm sorry' and started to beat a hasty retreat – but he starts talking again. All the time towelling himself off, drying between his toes – spraying himself with body spray. He starts getting dressed – blue boxers. White socks, white shirt – clean, ironed. Chest hairs curling underneath it. I tell you, people pay out to see men strip off – I tell you – this was a whole load more sexy. (*He stops and smiles – and becomes aware that the others are expecting more.*) That's it really.

KEVIN: What happened next?

MARTIN: He gave me a pop tart and I went home.

ROBERT: You mean you didn't do the business?

KEVIN: I thought you said he was the love of your life?

MARTIN: He was – but no, that didn't start later, until the bonfire night. (*Light dawns.*) Shit – did they want a shagging story? It's just they said they wanted to hear when I'd been the most aroused –

KEVIN: I wouldn't worry mate.

MARTIN: I could've told them a shagging story if they'd said – but to be perfectly honest none of them are half as good as that one. Or as long. Not the Mr Fly-Mo ones – the five minutes' wonder, God rot his socks. Anyway that was my story. And I managed to do the business. I guess that was the main thing. Everyone else manage to whack one out then? (*Everyone looks embarrassed apart from CRAIG.*) I thought the box of Kleenex looked a tad on the empty side. How long before they tell us if we've got in d'you reckon?

CRAIG: Couple of days – they've a few more to see –

MARTIN: I wouldn't have thought they'd be queueing round the block.

CRAIG: Then they need to go over the auditionees – look at personalities, profiles – see who works best together as a group –

MARTIN: Oh, puh-lease.

CRAIG: What?

MARTIN: This isn't fucking *Les Miserables.*

CRAIG: I'm not with you –

MARTIN: Surely they're bound to have us –

CRAIG: You think?

MARTIN: Come on. Reasonably fit, not bad looking – the right side of forty – that puts us three up on those other fellas who were there.

CRAIG: There's a bit more to it than that. (*MARTIN howls like a dog.*) It's a complicated business –

MARTIN: Why? I mean not to disparage what you do – surely at the end of the day it's just bonking.

CRAIG: Bonking on camera.

MARTIN: So?

CRAIG: You ever fucked on camera before?

MARTIN: Well – apart from an incident with some Polaroids – (*KEVIN and ROBERT laugh.*) You want to see them. (*To CRAIG.*) Surely there can't be that much to it?

KEVIN: Tell me about this workshop day.

MARTIN: Workshop day?

ROBERT: They were saying about that –

KEVIN: Sort of rehearsal isn't it?

CRAIG: We did something similar on the Bad Brit Boy film. They have them where there's a load of newbies. Basically they want to give you some idea of what it's like to have sex on camera.

MARTIN: What – some sort of mass orgy? Calm down Martin –

CRAIG: Not before the shoot –

MARTIN: We've got to shag at some point –

CRAIG: Yeah and how many people d'you want to shag a second time?

MARTIN: Without wishing to sound in any way like 'Conceited of SE1', it all sounds like a bit of a waste of time to me.

CRAIG: Oh – so you know how to move your arse so it doesn't look like you're holding a road drill? Or how to snog with someone keeping both your dicks facing outwards? How to stop coming until they've got the cameras focused?

ROBERT: So come on then – does it feel – odd –

CRAIG: Does what feel odd?

ROBERT: Having sex in front of a camera –

CRAIG: Nothing *odd* about it. As I say: it's just a load of stop start stop start – and at the end of the day it's just sex. No big deal.

Blackout.

Scene Two

CRAIG stands in the middle of the stage speaking on his mobile.

CRAIG: No, that's fine. No, it's no trouble. I'm all set. No – I'm happy to do it. Listen, if you *could* pay cash – up front – later on if that's possible – two hundred we said. Great. Okay – see you later – (*He takes a deep breath.*) The keynote of the day is honesty –

He starts unpacking a bag with things for the workshop day – Twister, a bottle of water, a bottle of vodka, a box of tissues etc, etc. As he does so the others enter, and moving around him, independent of each other speak on their mobile phones.

MARTIN: Hello? – Oh, hi, this is Martin – the man from the pub – calling. It's about nine thirty – am – Saturday morning –

ROBERT: Hello? Hi –

MARTIN: We met last night? – Anyway I was somewhat otherwise engaged – but you did tell me if I wanted to, to give you a ring – and here I am – giving you a ring –

ROBERT: I'm arrived. Yep, car alarm set, crook lock on – (*Tries foot on the floor and pulls a face.*) Inoculations updated.

MARTIN: And I was just wondering if you weren't busy maybe we could maybe meet up later on?

ROBERT: No, we're not in the video warehouse – we're in the Mandela rooms –

MARTIN: Have a drink –

ROBERT: A community centre of some description –

MARTIN: Grab a bite to eat –

ROBERT: Somewhere scuzzy where good is done –

KEVIN: Hi, it's me –

MARTIN: I'm busy all day to day – I'm at work – but you can leave a message on my voice mail –

ROBERT: I just wanted to remind you to pick up the dry cleaning – my jacket and your grey suit –

KEVIN: I was just phoning to say 'Hey – I love you' – As ready as I'll ever be.

ROBERT: Pinned on the cork notice board –

KEVIN: And if that guy from *Family Affairs* should call make sure you give him my mobile number again –

MARTIN: 07950 464873 – okay – give us a ring –

KEVIN: In case he's lost it –

ROBERT: I'd better go – I can see moulded plastic chairs being arranged –

MARTIN: I'll speak to you later (*Exits.*)

ROBERT: I will – love you too – (*Exits.*)

KEVIN: Love you too – see you later – (*Exits.*)

Having set everything out, CRAIG starts to get ready – put on body spray, comb his hair as he practises his speech. He speaks hesitantly; he's obviously just learnt it – sometimes as he reads he refers to his notes.

CRAIG: Okay – the object of us talking today – and the exercises we do – is to make you get to know each other a bit better – get more relaxed with each other. The more comfortable we are with each other, the better the sex – and let's face it, that's what the punters are going to be paying their fifteen quid for – good sex. If I had to sum up the day in one word: I'd say honesty –

ROBERT enters.

ROBERT: Hello Glorious Leader –

CRAIG: Hi –

ROBERT: Trainer as well as star – I'm impressed.

CRAIG: (*Flirting.*) The key word is honesty –

ROBERT: (*Responding.*) I'd better watch myself –

CRAIG: Not too hard –

ROBERT: How was it the other week? The Yard.

CRAIG: As ever – you know –

ROBERT: Unfortunately I don't – know that is –

CRAIG: You should try it.

ROBERT: I know I should –

CRAIG: Is that a 'but' I sense coming up?

ROBERT: But –

CRAIG: That wasn't so painful was it?

ROBERT: I'm a good boy –

CRAIG: Are you now? I think you'd really like it there –

ROBERT: Raunchy and sweaty?

CRAIG: Like I said – as ever. Excuse me. (*He moves away, breaking the moment.*)

Left alone ROBERT looks around, a look of disgust on his face. He whips out some Mr Muscle and a cloth from his bag. CRAIG is arranging the chairs. KEVIN approaches him.

KEVIN: Oh – hi –

CRAIG: Kevin – hi –

KEVIN: So you're running the day I hear –

CRAIG: I am indeed –

KEVIN: You all set?

CRAIG: Just about –

KEVIN: Only I was wondering – I know these really good breathing exercises – I mean really good – make you feel really energised –

CRAIG: I'll bear that in mind – (*Smiles.*)

KEVIN: So is it just exercises and games like?

CRAIG: And talking –

KEVIN: Right –

CRAIG: The keynote of the day is honesty –

KEVIN: So none of the actual business –

CRAIG: You mean shagging?

KEVIN: Yes.

CRAIG: I hadn't planned on it.

KEVIN: Not that I mind – no skin off my nose – only I'd just like to know – so I can psych myself up as it were.

CRAIG: I'm sure if you want someone'll oblige.

KEVIN: Hey, don't tempt me – seriously though –

CRAIG: There will be a certain amount of stripping off if that's all right.

KEVIN: That's fine.

CRAIG: You're okay with that?

KEVIN: No problem.

CRAIG: And the film?

KEVIN: Hey – it's just a job –

CRAIG: And Jess?

KEVIN: What about her?

CRAIG: She still cool about it?

KEVIN: Why shouldn't she be? She's fine – really supportive. After all –

CRAIG: It's just a job. Excuse me. (*He moves away.*)

Left alone KEVIN bursts into frenetic action, tearing off his trousers and rather staid boxer shorts. From out of his bag he produces a cellophane wrapped package. He tears open the bag and pulls out a pair of rather more raunchy CKs and puts them on. He stuffs his boxers and the wrappings back in his bag. CRAIG sets out a bottle and some plastic glasses as MARTIN approaches him.

MARTIN: Bridlington –

CRAIG: What?

MARTIN: Bridlington – Brid. Your home town. I knew I knew that accent – one of the guys was telling me. We had a caravan there see – 1986 to 1992. Sewerby Park. I know, how sad is that –

CRAIG: Good for you –

MARTIN: (*Not noticing his lack of enthusiasm.*) I know it's the Capital of the Planet Naff, but I used to love it there. The harbour – the Pavilion – I was the world crazy golf champion me. I even went there once with Mr Fly-Mo. (*Remembering.*) Sat on the front eating chips. Watching the ships out at sea. Then off for a bit of hot lurvin' down in the cliffs. Cue piano, Trevor Howard and Celia Johnson. (*He smiles, remembering.*)

CRAIG: Excuse me – (*Moves away.*)

MARTIN: So d'you get back there much?

CRAIG: No.

Cut to: CRAIG talking to the three others sat round on the chairs. This time the speech is polished and smooth.

CRAIG: If I had to sum up the day on one word: I'd say honesty – the whole object of us talking today – and the exercises we're going to do – is to make you get to know each other a bit better – get more relaxed with each other. The more comfortable we are with each other, the better the sex is going to be – and we might as well face it: that's what the punters are going to be paying their twenty nine ninety nine for. Bloody good sex.

MARTIN: I suppose it's a bit like a date really –

CRAIG: Sorry?

KEVIN: How?

MARTIN: Well with us – I mean it's no different from me and Stuart tonight – Leather Jacket Man – we'll be getting to know each other like we are today. Sex a definite possibility. I mean what's that if it's not a date? Sorry shut up Martin.

CRAIG: There's one crucial difference between this film and a date –

MARTIN: What's that then?

CRAIG: We get to shag whether we get on or not.

MARTIN: A case of eff ee eff ee –

CRAIG: What?

MARTIN: Fuck 'em forget 'em. Cheers. (*He takes a swig of his drink.*)

The men jump up, put the chairs to one side and take off their shirts so they're in their trousers and tee shirts, as CRAIG explains the game to them.

CRAIG: It's just like regular tag. One person's on – and when you're caught you freeze – you can only be freed.

MARTIN: I know – when someone goes between your legs –

CRAIG: Squeezes your cock actually. Hence the name: Squeeze Ball Tag –

MARTIN: Sorry – can I just ask a question?

CRAIG: Sure.

MARTIN: Why are we doing this?

For an answer CRAIG walks deliberately up to him and squeezes his balls. MARTIN flinches.

CRAIG: That's why. You got to get used to not flinching –

Freeze as KEVIN breaks and speaks into this mobile.

KEVIN: (*Into his mobile. As he speaks MARTIN, CRAIG and ROBERT take their trousers off.*) Jess? Hi – it's me – good – how's your day been? Excellentay. Listen, no calls for me? Right. Well no, not *definitely.* Definitely maybe. The workshop? (*The others take their trousers off.*) Okay – as speech and movement workshops go. All speech. And movement. Saying things – doing things. All very dull and boring but got to be done. (*He catches sight of the others without their trousers.*) Okay – I'd better go – love you –

Cut to: MARTIN, ROBERT and CRAIG are playing Twister – without their trousers on. KEVIN is calling out.

MARTIN: This is getting very exciting here.

ROBERT: Easy tiger.

CRAIG: Just call it out –

KEVIN: Sorry – right – right foot blue –

MARTIN: Pardon?

CRAIG: He said right foot blue –

MARTIN: I can't do that –

CRAIG: Just try –

MARTIN does – and the three come toppling over. CRAIG in doing so cracks his knee, ROBERT bangs his elbow, MARTIN his head. All three pretend they're not hurt.

MARTIN: Sorry folks –

CRAIG: It's all right –

ROBERT: Nil problemmo –

KEVIN: Is anyone hurt? (*They all deny this.*)

MARTIN: Are you sure Craig?

CRAIG: Yes.

MARTIN: You went with an awful crack on that knee –

CRAIG: It's fine, don't fuss. (*They all look a bit startled at this tone.*) – That knee's always a bit dodgy –

Cut to: The men are sitting in a circle. By now they're all holding drinks. This time KEVIN is talking.

KEVIN: (*Taking his trousers off.*) For me sex – with a woman – is about Spontaneity – No set rules, no set times or places – it's very much as and when the mood strikes – and speaking as a heterosexual, it's as much about the giving of pleasure as the receiving of it. A two-way street, definitely – but then I'm sure it is with gay blokes as well –

MARTIN: So you mean to say Kev, you're not attracted to us men at all?

KEVIN: Nothing personal mate. (*Laughs.*) I mean I can look at a man and think – 'He's nice' – you know – admire his figure – but that's as far as it goes. And okay, I know what you're thinking; you're thinking what planet is he on? But like I keep saying – to me this is just a job –

MARTIN: And what does Jess think about all this?

KEVIN: Why should she think anything?

ROBERT: It's just a job –

KEVIN: Right –

MARTIN: So she knows about this?

KEVIN: Of course.

MARTIN: And she doesn't mind?

KEVIN: Of course not – like when I did *Dolly Mixtures* at the Abattoir – she didn't think I was going to start fancying little girls – or at least I hope she didn't –

MARTIN: And sex with her is okay? Sorry I'm being really nosy here.

KEVIN: It's the best. It's the little touches. Body oils. Scented candles.

He nervously adjusts his collar. CRAIG hands him the vodka. He takes a cautious sip. Freeze as the men freeze and ROBERT breaks, speaking into his mobile.

ROBERT: Fine. It's going well. Of course not – it's only eleven o'clock – anyway, that's not the idea. Finding out the lie of the land. The nuts and bolts as t'were –

Five. Yes, I'll come straight home. Yes I know, don't worry. Fresh not frozen. And he drinks red, I know. I keep saying – we're not going to today. That's not part of the plan.

Cut to: The men sat in the group. This time ROBERT is talking.

ROBERT: Basically we like the high life, Marcus and myself – well we've got the money so why the hell not – good restaurants, fine wine, nice cars – things like that… when we fly we always fly club class – (*He smiles.*) You said you wanted to hear things about our sex lives – well that's one of our biggest thrills: tossing each other off Club Class –

MARTIN: The mile high club –

ROBERT: Once just across the aisle from Michael Portillo –

CRAIG: So if you had to rate the sex on a scale of one to –

MARTIN: (*Breaking in.*) – so how does your partner feel about you being in this film?

ROBERT: He's all for it –

MARTIN: He doesn't mind?

ROBERT: Why should he? He knows how I feel about him; I'm not about to go anywhere – it's a very relaxed relationship –

CRAIG: And if you had to rate the sex on a scale of one to ten?

ROBERT: Eight. And a half.

CRAIG: Good sex.

ROBERT: (*Looking him full on, smiling faintly.*) Good sex.

CRAIG: (*Smiling back.*) Good for you.

MARTIN: And he's really okay with you shagging someone else?

ROBERT: Course he is – like I say – he's very relaxed about that sort of thing.

CRAIG: Thank you, Robert. As I've said before – real sex might feel okay but that doesn't mean to say it looks okay on camera – so what you've got to learn is how to do it so it can be seen – and look the business.

MARTIN: Er –

CRAIG: (*Patiently.*) Yes –

MARTIN: At the risk of being totally boring – surely if you *like* each other – it'll all take care of itself.

ROBERT: Awww –

CRAIG: There's a bit more to it than that – (*By now they are wearing just their pants.*)

KEVIN: Isn't it all acting – and it's like the actor's job to communicate that to the audience –

CRAIG: Pretty hard if all the audience can see is half your arse and a crumpled duvet –

MARTIN: Surely that depends on the arse –

ROBERT: Get him –

CRAIG: Also it doesn't always *feel* good. Sexually. I mean it's hardly the biggest turn on, holding your arse in the air for ten minutes while someone gets the lighting right – but you've got to look as if you're having the top of your head blown off –

MARTIN: So how do you do that? (*For an answer CRAIG comes and sits on his knee – and groans touching his crotch.*)

ROBERT: Wow –

CRAIG: (*Breaking, instantly businesslike.*) That's how.

MARTIN: I suppose it's a bit like cookery books. (*They all look at him puzzled.*)

ROBERT: (*Laughing.*) What?

CRAIG: I'm not with you.

MARTIN: Like pictures of food in cookery books – it has to be specially arranged. And they put all sorts of gook in it to make it look nice on camera. I suppose no one wants to see a load of clumsy bonking any more than they want to see Delia served up on plastic plates – sorry, shall I shut up Martin.

Cut to: The men practising positions, etc.

CRAIG: Okay – and action –

ROBERT: Do you like that? (*MARTIN and KEVIN start to speak at the same time.*)

MARTIN: Sorry –

KEVIN: After you –

CRAIG: (*Impatiently.*) Don't stop – (*They move.*) Good – Think hot and horny – (*They continue, getting faster.*)

ROBERT: Do you like that?

MARTIN: That feels great – I like your pants.

ROBERT: I got them in New York.

KEVIN: Oh yes! (*They all look at him in surprise.*) Sorry lads – just getting into character –

MARTIN: Ow –

CRAIG: Keep going – (*The three suddenly break.*)

MARTIN: This is killing my knees –

CRAIG: Fuck your knees – keep going –

MARTIN: It's really hurting –

CRAIG: So what'll you do on film –

MARTIN: It's hardly fucking erotic –

CRAIG: So? (*MARTIN groans.*) Keep going – faster –
(*KEVIN suddenly breaks.*)

KEVIN: God – I'm really sorry –

CRAIG: What?

KEVIN: It must've been that curry last night. (*By now they've all caught a whiff.*) Really sorry lads.

Cut to: CRAIG is talking to the group as they get dressed.

CRAIG: Okay, here's the script for you to take away and read at your leisure –

MARTIN: Who gets to shag me –

CRAIG: Okay – just to summarise the pairings – Kevin you get to go with myself and with Robert –

KEVIN: Oh – right –

CRAIG: Is that okay?

KEVIN: Sure – pushing back the frontiers of gay / straight collaboration –

CRAIG: Robert you're with myself and Kevin obviously – plus you have a solo jerk off session.

ROBERT: Wa-hay.

CRAIG: Which leaves Martin: you get to go with me –

MARTIN: Just you –

CRAIG: Just me – is that okay? (*ROBERT laughs.*)

KEVIN: What?

ROBERT: You wait till you see page seventy-two mate –

CRAIG: Okay – if I can bring it to a close here – you've all got the script – obviously you need to learn it and familiarise yourself with your part – are there any questions? Basically is everyone happy?

ROBERT: (*Still chortling away.*) I'm fine mate –

KEVIN: Yeah –

CRAIG: Martin? Any problems?

MARTIN: No –

CRAIG: Great –

MARTIN: Not as such.

CRAIG: As you know the shoot's on the sixteenth – come expecting a long, boring day –

ROBERT: A hard day –

CRAIG: A hard day – and of course get the script learnt.

ROBERT and KEVIN go to their things, MARTIN makes to follow them.

Martin – can I have a quick word?

MARTIN: Can I just check my voice mail?

CRAIG: This won't take a minute.

MARTIN: Okay.

CRAIG: It's just this: if there are any problems – I need to tell the producer now.

MARTIN: Problems?

CRAIG: Problems.

MARTIN: So are there?

CRAIG: You tell me.

MARTIN: Do I look like I've got a problem?

CRAIG: To be honest: yes.

MARTIN: What?

CRAIG: For one thing you don't seem to be taking it very seriously.

MARTIN: Take what?

CRAIG: Today –

MARTIN: Today –

CRAIG: Yes –

MARTIN: Trouserless Twister, Squeeze Ball Tag –

CRAIG: I said why we were doing those things –

MARTIN: Okay – hands in the air – I'm sorry. The next time we play games with no trousers on I'll be totally and utterly serious. Can I go now Sir?

CRAIG: Hang on a sec –

MARTIN: What –

CRAIG: You may as well come out and say it –

MARTIN: Say what?

CRAIG: That you're not keen on the idea of having sex with me.

MARTIN: I didn't say that –

CRAIG: If it makes you feel any better I don't particularly want to have sex with you –

MARTIN: Thanks a bunch –

CRAIG: It's nothing personal – you're not my type – like I'm not yours. But if you did the film – I'd have to be. You'd have to be fucked by me – and you'd have to look as though you were enjoying it – you'd have to look as though it was the best fuck you'd ever had in your life. It can be done. It can be done – but it's not for everyone.

A pause.

You said on your audition tape – you wanted to do this to meet someone –

MARTIN: I'm not going to fall head over heels in love with you if that's what's worrying you.

CRAIG: If you are going to do this, you're going to have to make a compartment in your head.

MARTIN: And is that what you do?

CRAIG: Yes it is.

MARTIN: Sex is sex, love is love, never the twain shall meet?

CRAIG: Not in a porn film.

MARTIN: So no one you have sex with you're ever going to fall for?

CRAIG: Not on a shoot.

MARTIN: Or even feel anything for?

CRAIG: No –

MARTIN: I see –

CRAIG: I think you need to think about it very carefully. (*He turns to go.*)

MARTIN: Don't you ever get scared?

CRAIG: (*It's clear he hasn't expected this.*) Scared?

MARTIN: Scared you'll lose the knack of having a relationship –

CRAIG: No, why should I?

MARTIN: So if you wanted to take something further – d'you think you could?

CRAIG: But I wouldn't want to.

MARTIN: But if you did – say if you wanted to ask out Kev, or Rob maybe –

CRAIG: I wouldn't want to do that –

MARTIN: Just suppose for argument's sake you did – d'you think you could?

CRAIG: Of course I could –

MARTIN: And you think they'd say yes?

CRAIG: I wouldn't really care one way or the other –

MARTIN: I mean after what you've said about yourself today?

CRAIG: What?

MARTIN: (*Quoting.*) 'For me sex is about excitement – energy. Why go to the valleys when you've had the mountain peaks?'

CRAIG: We're not talking about me – we're talking about you and whether you should be in this film. I need to let the producers know –

MARTIN: Can I make a compartment in my head?

CRAIG: Yes.

MARTIN: Can I be shagged by you and look like it's the best thing since sliced bread even though I don't particularly like you –

CRAIG: You don't have to make your mind up now – think about it – call the producers –

MARTIN: Okay, I will think about it – whilst I'm having my date with a handsome guy who I approached – who wants to take me out for a drink – with whom I may or may not have rampant unphotogenic rumpy pumpy with – I will think about this question – (*He goes out – CRAIG kicks the chair.*)

Cut to: CRAIG stands on his own. ROBERT enters carrying his bag.

ROBERT: Everything okay?

CRAIG: Yeah, fine –

ROBERT: I'm just off. Thanks for an enlightening day –

CRAIG: You survived –

ROBERT: Just about – no, I enjoyed it. Very informative. Anyway –

CRAIG: Listen: I don't know about you – but I'm gagging for a drink –

ROBERT: Ah –

CRAIG: I just wondered if you fancied a quick beer.

ROBERT: No can do I'm afraid –

CRAIG: It's okay –

ROBERT: Prior engagement and all that –

CRAIG: It's all right.

ROBERT: We've these people coming over for dinner – some old friends of ours. They're going over to their place in Antigua for Christmas – so Christmas is tonight.

CRAIG: Noel.

ROBERT: Bit of a drag – but then that's Coupledom –

CRAIG: See you.

ROBERT exits.

KEVIN enters.

KEVIN: I'm just off.

CRAIG: Okay day?

KEVIN: (*Jokingly.*) Speaking as a 'red blooded heterosexual' – fine –

CRAIG: I hope it wasn't too threatening? – Speaking as a red-blooded homosexual.

KEVIN: No, not at all –

CRAIG: Just a job –

KEVIN: No different to acting a rescue man – or a policeman –

CRAIG: So when you research something like that – d'you spend some time at a police station?

KEVIN: Ideally – or at watching *The Bill* –

CRAIG: Well if you fancy some more research – I'm off to a gay bar now – if you wanted to come along.

KEVIN: Ah –

CRAIG: See how the other half lives –

KEVIN: Thing is mate – Jess and I – we're going out for a meal –

CRAIG: Fair enough –

KEVIN: Sort of Christmas thing. There's this Thai place we go to – 'All you can eat' buffet –

CRAIG: It's okay –

KEVIN: Another time –

CRAIG: Sure.

KEVIN: Okay then. See you –

CRAIG: See you. (*KEVIN exits. CRAIG stands alone.*)

Cut to: Some gay club ferocious disco beat. Again CRAIG stands alone. He seems to be brooding. MARTIN comes up to him.

47

MARTIN: Hi there – (*CRAIG looks at him.*) It's fairly hopping tonight –

CRAIG: I didn't think I'd see you here. (*He sounds pissed.*)

MARTIN: I'm sure you didn't.

CRAIG: So where's the drop dead gorgeous Stuart then?

MARTIN: The drop dead gorgeous Stuart is not here. The drop dead gorgeous Stuart has left the building. Except the bastard never entered it in the first place.

CRAIG: He didn't ring.

MARTIN: Cue violins. Only I think I've had a lucky escape. And before you say anything – I think you're absolutely right – I mean in a porn film there's none of this *shit* – none of this waiting and hanging around and feeling a twat. *And* you get paid for the privilege.

CRAIG: So you're on your own.

MARTIN: Like I said – cue violins –

CRAIG: D'you want another?

MARTIN: Why not?

CRAIG goes off smiling. It's not a nice smile.

Blackout.

Scene Three

CRAIG stands in the centre, reading a letter. As he does the others come on. Each has something with them that they use throughout the scene. CRAIG has weights with which he works out. KEVIN brings incense sticks and a candle and sits as if meditating. ROBERT is polishing a candlestick. MARTIN brings on a can, which he slumps down with. Each has their script, at which they glance throughout.

CRAIG: (*Reading.*) As you know the day of the shoot is Saturday December 16th. Between now and then you need to find the time to read the script, familiarise yourself with the role – and of course learn your lines. Hopefully the story avoids clichés and tells a story that is both quirky and relevant to the everyday situation of gay men –

Hot Shooting Guys 2:

Craig will be playing the part of Carl – twenty-three, a young attractive twink ready to find out about his body.

Kevin will be playing the part of Horse –

KEVIN: (*Reading.*) A man Carl meets in the sauna –

CRAIG: A horny stud always ready for a shag –

KEVIN: (*To himself.*) Feel the truth, feel the truth –

CRAIG: Robert will be playing the part of Mic –

ROBERT: (*Spelling it out.*) M – i – c…

CRAIG: – a raunchy mechanic who sees to Carl's motor –

ROBERT: – and to Carl –

CRAIG: He likes it dirty – the dirtier the better. And finally Martin'll be playing the part of Ben –

MARTIN: I mean how Enid Blyton is *that* –

CRAIG: Early twenties – cheerful, straightforward and uncomplicated –

MARTIN: That's me.

CRAIG: Never thinking further than the next shag.

Reading from the script.

Carl's flat on the ground floor of a large terraced south London house. The house is well-decorated throughout –

ROBERT: Surely – decorated well?

CRAIG: – in a colourful blend of the tasteful and colourful – there is evidence of both money and style. Early morning. Summer. It's going to be a hot day. The radio can be heard saying the temperature is due to soar to the sizzling nineties –

ROBERT: Classic FM is this?

CRAIG: Sun streams in through the well-appointed windows –

Cut to CRAIG's flat. There is an instant sound of rain and wind, heavy, insistent. CRAIG and MARTIN enter, togged up against the weather. CRAIG especially is a bit the worse for drink. He turns on lamps, music, the gas.

MARTIN: (*Who is stood in the middle of the room.*) Very nice. Love these Victorian attics.

CRAIG: Drink?

MARTIN: D'you not think we've had enough?

CRAIG: Vodka or vodka?

MARTIN: You've not got any coffee?

CRAIG: No –

MARTIN: No coffee.

CRAIG: No coffee, just vodka. (*He takes an ecstasy tablet.*)

MARTIN: How long have you been here?

CRAIG: Six months.

MARTIN: And London?

CRAIG: Long enough – (*Puts music on.*)

MARTIN: You've not much stuff –

CRAIG: Stuff?

MARTIN: Furniture – posters – things –

CRAIG: You mean shite.

MARTIN: No. So you get back much?

CRAIG: Back?

MARTIN: Bridlington.

CRAIG: No –

MARTIN: Never?

CRAIG: Why the fuck should I?

MARTIN: Sorry –

CRAIG: You've got some romantic idea of it being my home by the sea – it isn't. It's just a place I used to live. And I live here now.

He brandishes the vodka. MARTIN nods. CRAIG smiles, steps forward. Kisses MARTIN, gropes him. MARTIN breaks.

MARTIN: You got a loo?

CRAIG: Through there on the right –

MARTIN exits. CRAIG takes another drink and turns up the music.

Sound cuts. Cut back to the men reading the script.

MARTIN: (*Obviously pissed off.*) Carl lies on the bed, a sheet covering and revealing the outlines of his body –

CRAIG: Thighs, calves, buttocks, belly – (*As he speaks MARTIN goes and picks up his mobile and stares at trying to decide whether to ring or not.*)

KEVIN: Obviously he works out at the gym.

CRAIG: Obviously –

ROBERT: He stirs, blinking at the sun shining into his eyes.

KEVIN: He pushes off the sheet and goes to close the blind –

ROBERT: We see his body outlined against the window –

KEVIN: Thighs, calves, belly –

CRAIG: (*Impatient.*) Yeah yeah yeah – (*MARTIN throws the phone down.*)

KEVIN: Tight white briefs over taut sculpted buttocks –

CRAIG: He starts to play with himself – as you do – rubbing and wanking harder and harder –

Flashback.

GRAHAM'S VOICE: Having a wank are you?

CRAIG: Graham – fuck's sake –

GRAHAM: Your Mum said I could up –

CRAIG: Fucking hell –

GRAHAM: Come on, Craigy –

CRAIG: What?

GRAHAM: Come on – get out of bed you fucking lazy article –

CRAIG: Piss off –

GRAHAM: Hey – you were the one wanting to go for a run –

CRAIG: What?

GRAHAM: Sewerby Park – twice round – come on you lazy arsehole –

CRAIG: (*To drown out the memory.*) Rubbing and wanking –

KEVIN: Harder and harder –

ROBERT: Free hand running over his body –

CRAIG: (*Sombre.*) Buttocks, belly, thighs and calves –

MARTIN: Moaning he starts to come –

CRAIG stares ahead – and snaps back to the flat. He takes a swig of his drink and goes to refill MARTIN's glass.

CRAIG: So –

MARTIN: So – (*CRAIG kisses him.*) I was thinking –

CRAIG: Thinking what?

MARTIN: Maybe I should go –

CRAIG: Anyone ever tell you you talk too much?

MARTIN: Probably best –

CRAIG: Not from where I'm standing –

MARTIN: You want me to stay?

CRAIG: That depends what you think this is –

MARTIN: I don't know – it's…something –

CRAIG: No –

MARTIN: No?

CRAIG: No. No it's not something. It's nothing. Nothing at all. Fuck all – if you'll pardon the expression. (*Kisses him again.*) Except –

MARTIN: Except what?

CRAIG: Except I was able to ask someone out for a drink – and they, knowing full well who I am and what I think and what I was offering – said yes –

MARTIN: You mean –

CRAIG: This is nothing more than a meaningless shag – (*They kiss – at that second the tape slurs and stops.*) Fuck –

MARTIN: What?

CRAIG has hurried over to the machine and opened the case. A spool of tape spills out.

CRAIG: Fuck fuck fuck –

Cut back to the men reading the script.

KEVIN: Mic's garage.

ROBERT: Half dismantled cars, oil on the floor –

CRAIG: Carl enters –

KEVIN: Carl:

CRAIG: Hello?

KEVIN: Mic enters with a smudge of grease on his face.

CRAIG: Mic:

ROBERT: Hello.

KEVIN: Carl:

CRAIG: Any news on the motor mate?

ROBERT: Bad news mate, it's going to cost you more than
you thought.

KEVIN: Carl:

CRAIG: Oh no.

KEVIN: Mic:

ROBERT: Big end's gone see, I need to get a part in. It's
going to cost I'm afraid.

CRAIG: Oh shit –

ROBERT: What is it mate?

CRAIG: I'm a bit skint till my grant comes through.

ROBERT: The work will have to wait then.

CRAIG: But I really need the motor.

ROBERT: Well – there's more than one way to pay.

CRAIG: What had you in mind?

Flashback:

ROBERT sputters.

MR WALTON: What?

ROBERT: It's gone up my nose –

MR WALTON: What are we going to do with you – come here –

ROBERT: It's nice –

MR WALTON: Some come on –

ROBERT: What? (*Knowing full weel what.*)

MR WALTON: Don't I get a proper thank you?

ROBERT: Thank you Mr Walton –

MR WALTON: You can't turn thirteen and not try champagne –

ROBERT: Thank you very much – (*Raunchy music continues.*)

CRAIG: What had you in mind?

ROBERT: Mic clutches his dick through his suit trousers.

CRAIG: Carl smiles and rubs his nipple.

KEVIN: He moans slightly.

CRAIG: Ooohhh –

ROBERT: I'll show you how you can pay me college boy –

MARTIN: Mic pulls Carl towards him –

KEVIN: He expertly undoes his trousers and gets his dick out –

MARTIN: Carl moans –

CRAIG: Mmmmm

KEVIN: Mic begins to suck –

MARTIN: As Carl strips his top off –

KEVIN: Mic gets his own dick out –

ROBERT: (*Mouth full.*) How much are you going to pay then college boy?

KEVIN: He pushes Carl over the bonnet of the car and parts his taut cheeks.

CRAIG: Give me your big end motor man –

KEVIN: Mic enters Carl and begins to pump his hardened cock in and out of his tight welcoming rosebud –

ROBERT: He slaps Carl's arse –

CRAIG: Ow –

ROBERT: You'll pay all right college boy –

MARTIN: He continues pumping –

ROBERT: In, out, in, out – in – out –

ROBERT stands alone in a spotlight holding the candlestick.

CRAIG: Saturday mornings.

MARTIN: Early morning –

KEVIN: Light showing pink behind the curtains.

CRAIG: The noise of traffic on the main road.

ROBERT: He lies there. Doesn't say anything. Presses his thigh against mine. Touches me, makes me hard.

KEVIN: Go on then.

ROBERT: I get up, get out of bed.

CRAIG: Second drawer down.

MARTIN: Football shirt and shorts.

ROBERT: I put them on, all the time touching myself.

KEVIN: God, you're beautiful –

ROBERT: When did he get so fat – and white?

KEVIN: Come here –

ROBERT: I lie on the bed, face down, arse pointing in the air. Hands shaking he pulls my shorts down. Like a kid unwrapping a present on Christmas morning. He exhales, kisses my backside.

KEVIN: God, I want to fuck you –

ROBERT: And when he's done he kisses my face, forcing his tongue in.

KEVIN: I love you –

ROBERT: I know why people close their eyes when they kiss. It's so they can pretend they're with someone else.

Cut back to the flat. MARTIN is totally absorbed in mending the tape with that concentration and attention that can seem really sexy.

MARTIN: That's it – you just need to rewind it –

CRAIG: Thanks –

MARTIN: Careful – don't snag it – you got a screwdriver?

CRAIG: I don't think so –

MARTIN: Never mind – I can manage with this – (*Uses a knife to fiddle with the machine.*) Ah – thought so –

CRAIG: What is it?

MARTIN: The tape heads are going out of alignment – it's a common thing in tapes as they get older –

CRAIG: It's not that old –

MARTIN: Hardly what you'd call state of the art though is it? I mean I thought you'd have the latest DVD digital downloadable whatsit.

CRAIG: Did you –

MARTIN: The rollers need cleaning – all you need is a cotton bud dipped in meths – hold it against the rollers and press play.

CRAIG: Thanks.

MARTIN: Just call me Mr Fix-It. (*A pause.*) The thing is – with you – I'm nervous –

CRAIG: Sorry?

MARTIN: Nervous.

CRAIG: Nervous.

MARTIN: Of you.

CRAIG: I don't know what you're talking about.

MARTIN: I'm not a porn star –

CRAIG: So?

MARTIN: Or even a Chippendale.

CRAIG: What the fuck are you going on about Martin?

MARTIN: 'Why go to the valleys when you've had the mountain peaks?' There's no way I'd measure up to that – I'd be thinking all the time – you know – how am I looking – what should I say – is my arse in the right place? (*He sits. CRAIG sits down where he is. A pause.*)

CRAIG: Your arse looks fine to me. (*A pause. Then, not looking at him.*) The Chippendale was crap if you must know. (*They look at each other and half smile. MARTIN takes his hand.*)

Cut back to the men reading the script.

ROBERT: Carl sits in the sauna. Hot wet steam strokes his taut ready body.

KEVIN: Enter Horse.

CRAIG: Tall, fit, and gagging for it –

KEVIN: (*Doing acting exercises.*) Find the anger – find the anger –

ROBERT: He sees Carl and looks.

KEVIN: And looks away –

CRAIG: And looks –

KEVIN: And looks away.

ROBERT: Horse looks and smiles. Carl looks and smiles.

KEVIN: Breath – breath – find the anger –

ROBERT: Horse:

KEVIN: Hey –

ROBERT: Carl:

CRAIG: Hey –

ROBERT: Horse:

KEVIN: You want to go down on my big piece of meat?

CRAIG: Sure –

ROBERT: Horse touches his hardening dick. Carl touches his hardening dick.

KEVIN: Breathe, breathe – find the anger – find the anger –

Flashback:

DAD: Go on –

KEVIN: I can't –

DAD: Course you can – you're not trying – come on –

KEVIN: Like this?

DAD: No – with the tips of the fingers – that's it – now…run up…come on – And…no – *overarm*…the arm goes up –

KEVIN: Can we go back now?

DAD: We cannot –

KEVIN: I'll miss *New Faces.*

DAD: You want to watch yourself – bloody jessie –

CRAIG: Carl smiles and squeezes his, by now, fully erect shaft. Horse crosses them room, his enormous erect member in his hand –

KEVIN: How's about you suck my dick college boy?

CRAIG: Sure thing mister. (*Sounding very bored with the whole thing.*) Carl takes Horse in his mouth and begins to suck –

KEVIN: (*Almost beside himself.*) Horse begins regular pumping rhythm – in out, in out, in out – (*He skims down the page.*) Shine on – (*Reading again.*) Yes yes yes – (*To himself.*) Breathe in – breathe out – find the anger, find the anger –

CRAIG: A room –

ROBERT: Dimly lit –

CRAIG: A smell of incense –

ROBERT: Music playing –

KEVIN: She sits, smiling. Hand touching her breast –

CRAIG: Kevin goes over –

KEVIN: Sits behind her –

MARTIN: Tentatively she puts a hand on his thigh –

KEVIN: Breathe in, breathe out –

CRAIG: Touches his –

ROBERT: Squeezes his dick –

KEVIN: Find the feeling, look inside and find the feeling –

MARTIN: I love you –

KEVIN: I love you too –

CRAIG: He kisses her fiercely –

ROBERT: Eyes closed tight –

KEVIN: Nothing but a mouth – a tongue – a body –

MARTIN: Aaah –

KEVIN: It could be anyone – anyone –

CRAIG: She takes off her top –

ROBERT: Her breasts fall free –

KEVIN: Find the feeling – find the feeling –

> *Cut to the flat. MARTIN and CRAIG are lying down, post-coital. The rain pours down outside. Suddenly MARTIN sits bolt upright.*

CRAIG: What?

MARTIN: Sorry –

CRAIG: What is it?

MARTIN: Nothing. Bad dream. Too much booze.

CRAIG: You okay?

MARTIN: Yeah. Don't worry about it. You okay?

CRAIG: (*Sleepily.*) Yeah –

MARTIN: (*Rumpling his hair.*) Lived up to expectations then? (*CRAIG smiles and stretches.*) Better than the Chippendale then? It's still raining –

CRAIG: Yeah – (*They sit a minute, listening to the sound.*)

MARTIN: Who's Graham?

CRAIG: Sorry?

MARTIN: You said his name –

CRAIG: I dunno –

MARTIN: You told him to fuck off – (*CRAIG shrugs. He doesn't seem very disposed to talk about this any more. Pause. The noise of rain.*) When I was a kid – and it was raining at night – I'd pretend I was in a tent in the middle of a forest – and it was all cold and wet and dark outside – but inside I was like safe and warm and all snuggled up. D'you ever go camping as a kid?

CRAIG: No –

MARTIN: Never in the Scouts? Dib dib dib and all that?

CRAIG: No –

MARTIN: Parents still alive then?

CRAIG: The last I heard.

MARTIN: Still together?

CRAIG: As far as I know –

MARTIN: You not get on like?

CRAIG: We don't not get on. I just don't see that much of them.

MARTIN: So I take it you're not going home for Christmas?

CRAIG: No. (*He turns over and goes to sleep.*)

Cut back to the script.

ROBERT: Enter Ben – cheerful and uncomplicated.

MARTIN: (*Not sounding convinced.*) That's me.

ROBERT: Carl:

CRAIG: Who the fuck are you?

KEVIN: Ben:

MARTIN: Sorry mate, didn't mean to scare you.

ROBERT: Carl:

CRAIG: Who are you?

ROBERT: Ben:

MARTIN: I'm the electrician. I heard there's a plug gone.

CRAIG: Oh, that's right –

MARTIN: Where is it?

CRAIG: Where do you think mister –

Flashback:

MARTIN: In a box – at the top of the wardrobe – all tangled up, the wire twisted into knots – some of the bulbs gone… hurry hurry hurry – (*The lights dim, fairy lights appear.*) Done.

Music starts. Rosemary Clooney: 'Have Yourself a Merry Little Christmas'.

FLY-MO MAN: What's all this?

MARTIN: Happy Christmas – I won't see you again – so I thought I'd say Happy Christmas properly.

FLY-MO MAN: We need to keep it down –

MARTIN: Sorry. I got you this –

FLY-MO MAN: Oh – right – thanks. And that's great –

MARTIN: I missed you.

FLY-MO MAN: Look – I've not got you anything.

MARTIN: That's okay.

FLY-MO MAN: I missed you too – You make me so hard –

MARTIN: I love you –

FLY-MO MAN: Look, we've only got twenty minutes – Bev's taken the kids to a party –

MARTIN: Oh, right –

FLY-MO MAN: So are we going to fuck or what then?

CRAIG: It's over here –

MARTIN: Ben gets out a spanner –

CRAIG: That's a big tool –

MARTIN: I've got a bigger one than that college boy –

CRAIG: I reckon I'd like to see that –

MARTIN: Always happy to oblige a customer. (*The following read very passionately, but sadly – almost like a love poem – the tone making a nonsense of the words.*) Ben smiles. He pulls back the duvet.

CRAIG: Carl smiles welcomingly –

MARTIN: As Ben moves towards him.

CRAIG: He touches his nipples –

MARTIN: Hard belly –

CRAIG: Stiffening cock –

MARTIN: That's some dick –

CRAIG: He runs his tongue over his nipples –

MARTIN: Belly –

CRAIG: Thighs –

MARTIN: Suck my dick college boy –

CRAIG: Carl takes Ben's cock in his mouth and begins to suck –

MARTIN: Suck my cock college boy.

MARTIN and CRAIG stand separately in spotlights.

MARTIN: Asleep he looks so young –

CRAIG: His hair smells of shampoo –

MARTIN: His cheek creased on the pillow –

CRAIG: He's so *warm* –

MARTIN: Breathing slowly –

CRAIG: Breathing –

MARTIN: Don't wake up – don't wake up – don't wake up –

CRAIG: (*Harshly.*) Ben comes in Carl's face – (*MARTIN throws the script down.*)

Cut to the flat. Morning. CRAIG wakes. MARTIN is not there. CRAIG sits up, his expression unreadable. He lights up. MARTIN enters with a tray of breakfast.

MARTIN: Morning – (*He is carrying two mugs.*)

CRAIG: Oh – hi –

MARTIN: I helped myself, I hope you don't mind – I don't know whose coffee it was – I took a risk – milk, no sugar –

CRAIG: Actually I don't drink coffee.

MARTIN: Oh, sorry.

CRAIG: It doesn't matter –

MARTIN: Rain's stopped anyway –

CRAIG: Yes –

MARTIN: (*At the window.*) Nice view from here – you can see for miles. You'd never think London'd be so *green*. Hey, is that the Dome?

CRAIG: Probably. (*He starts to get dressed.*)

MARTIN: So what are you doing today?

CRAIG: I don't know. Going to the gym at some point.

MARTIN: I've a job on this morning – but maybe we can meet up for lunch?

CRAIG: I don't know.

MARTIN: Or later on –

CRAIG: I don't know what I'm doing –

MARTIN: Tonight? (*CRAIG doesn't respond. MARTIN goes to hold him – but he pulls away.*)

CRAIG: (*Breaking in.*) Actually I better get on.

MARTIN: Right –

CRAIG: You can see yourself out?

MARTIN: Yeah, right. Course. (*Pauses at the door.*) See you on the sixteenth then. Raring to go.

He exits. CRAIG sighs and sits. Looks at the breakfast tray.

Carl lies on the bed smiling, remembering the hot sex.

CRAIG is in fact standing alone expressionless. We hear the voices of the other men, not as themselves but memories from CRAIG's past.

ROBERT: A toilet – (*We hear the noise of the sea.*)

KEVIN: Small –

ROBERT: Graffiti –

KEVIN: Stinking of piss –

CRAIG: Next to the Pavilion.

MARTIN: Across from the crazy golf –

CRAIG: I'm not going in –

MARTIN: (*Insistently.*) A public toilet, small, stinking of piss, next to the Pavilion, across from the crazy golf.

CRAIG: Morning –

ROBERT: Dusk –

MARTIN: Always dusk –

CRAIG: Even in day time – I'm not going in – but I need a slash – there's nothing wrong with needing a slash –

MARTIN: Craig enters the toilet –

CRAIG: Men stood in the gloom –

KEVIN: Like ghosts –

ROBERT: A cold day –

CRAIG: I can see my breath –

MARTIN: A man in a suit –

CRAIG: Like someone you'd see in an office – or the bank – big brown briefcase. I've never seen him before. He must be from Lincoln or somewhere.

He looks – I look away but he's still looking. Staring. Fingering his cock.

MARTIN: Hi –

CRAIG: Hello –

MARTIN: Nice cock –

CRAIG: Yes –

MARTIN: I bet that gets hard. I bet you get hard.

CRAIG: I don't know really –

MARTIN: Come here then –

CRAIG: He takes me in a cubicle. Cold. Ice in the bowl. Black magic marker on the tiles.

MARTIN: What's wrong?

CRAIG: Nothing –

MARTIN: Go on then – bend over –

CRAIG: What'you doing – (*He's bent over by the man.*)

MARTIN: I'll just put this on – you want this –

CRAIG: Yes. In front of my eyes: 'Meet here for cock fun. Evenings after six' – (*He gasps in pain.*)

MARTIN: Keep it down for fuck's sake –

CRAIG: It hurts –

MARTIN: It's all right – relax – it won't hurt –

CRAIG: It is fucking hurting –

MARTIN: Shhhh – yes – does that feel good?

CRAIG: Yes –

MARTIN: You see – I knew it would – (*He starts to gasp as he comes.*) Oh baby! (*He gasps again – and pulls out.*)

CRAIG: Is that it?

MARTIN: I have to go –

CRAIG: Hang on –

MARTIN: See you around –

CRAIG: Wait –

MARTIN: What?

CRAIG: Can I see you again?

MARTIN: Not a good idea – (*He fades away.*)

CRAIG: The camera fades out through the window and pans down onto the street –

MARTIN: We focus in on Carl. Walking down the street, troubles over, basking in the sunshine. A man who knows what he likes and where he's going, confident in his self and his sexuality. He may not know what's round the corner but he's ready for it –

Blackout.

Scene Four

CRAIG stands expressionless in the middle of the stage with the script. Fade up the noise of confusion – hammering, talking, bursts of sound – as the shoot is prepared. CRAIG takes a drink, still expressionless. ROBERT and KEVIN walk on, a little bemused. ROBERT sips from a Starbucks Christmas cup. CRAIG 'switches on' becoming relaxed and confident.

KEVIN: Are we sure this is the right gaff?

ROBERT: (*As he walks on.*) I hope my car's going to be all right – (*They're both carrying Starbucks cups.*)

CRAIG: In here guys –

KEVIN: Hi –

ROBERT: It's the man –

CRAIG: How' you both doing? (*He hugs each one.*)

KEVIN: Good –

ROBERT: Yeah, great –

ROBERT and KEVIN look around the room, nervousness giving way to with distaste.

CRAIG: Raring to go?

KEVIN: Well –

ROBERT: Yes –

KEVIN: You know –

CRAIG: Here. (*He pours a slug from a bottle into their Starbucks cups.*) Drink up then – Cheers. (*They respond reluctantly.*)

KEVIN: It's a bit chilly in here –

CRAIG: They've been having trouble with the electrics – the heater only just came on – it'll soon warm up –

ROBERT: (*Looking round.*) So what happened to quote 'well appointed south London' unquote?

CRAIG: Welcome to well appointed South London – Friend of director's – gone to Gran Canaria for Christmas.

ROBERT: The script did say classy –

CRAIG: The script did say 'hot summer'. That's the joy and wonder of film making. (*He tops his drink up.*) Anyway, like I say, it'll soon warm up. (*KEVIN and ROBERT sit, both looking nervous.*) You okay then Rob?

ROBERT: Yes.

CRAIG: Kevin?

KEVIN: I'm fine.

CRAIG: Good. That's good. Well – here's to film making.

He touches ROBERT – and kisses him expertly on the neck. ROBERT relaxes. CRAIG kisses ROBERT. Looks at KEVIN.

You not joining us then?

KEVIN just looks. CRAIG kisses him. KEVIN nervously half responds.

You'll soon get the hang of it. Remember – it's just a job. (*He touches him – massages his neck.*) To the magic of the screen – (*He raises his glass. The others respond.*)

KEVIN: No sign of Martin yet then?

CRAIG: (*Smoothly still massaging.*) 'Fraid he's had to pull out –

ROBERT: Oh?

KEVIN: Pull out?

CRAIG: (*Leaving him.*) Happens all the time – he decided it wasn't for him –

ROBERT: I've been having serious doubts whether it's for me –

CRAIG: You'll be fine. (*Pours another slug into his cup.*)

ROBERT: So how long d'you reckon they'll be?

CRAIG: (*Pouring into his coffee.*) Not too long – hey, relax – (*He goes behind him.*) God, you're stiff –

ROBERT: Oh yes?

CRAIG: Yes – (*He starts to massage his neck. Robert relaxes.*)

ROBERT: God, that's good –

CRAIG: Better?

ROBERT: I'll say –

CRAIG: You want me to do you Kev? (*A pause.*)

KEVIN: Go on then –

CRAIG: Okay – hold my drink Robert – and top it up –

ROBERT: Sure thing –

CRAIG: There we go – how's that?

KEVIN: That's great –

MARTIN enters.

MARTIN: (*Brittle and nervous.*) Hi chaps –

ROBERT: Oh, hi Martin –

KEVIN: We were just talking about you –

MARTIN: No wonder my ears were burning. Well – here we are – four men about to shag the arses off each other. My God, so this is the glamour of show biz? Well – go on then – lead me to my trailer –

The mood being built up by CRAIG has been well and truly shattered.

ROBERT: I thought you'd pulled out –

MARTIN: As it were – no – rumours of my demise have been greatly exaggerated. No, I knew they'd have trouble finding someone else at such short notice – I can't let down the honour that is Overload Productions Inc – so I said I'd do it. Before you all get *too* carried away here, there's this extremely dodgy character in the kitchen who says he's here to do make up and can he have Horse and Mic so he can put talc on their arses –

KEVIN: Shite –

MARTIN: What have you got that I haven't we ask ourselves.

ROBERT: Now –

MARTIN: If not sooner.

KEVIN and ROBERT exit. MARTIN looks at CRAIG who ignores him and studies his script.

Well – don't I even get a hello?

CRAIG: Hello.

MARTIN: Hello. (*Pause.*) Well you might at least say it –

CRAIG: (*Looking at his script.*) Martin: I'm not going to say 'say what'?

MARTIN: Not even – 'I've been busy' – 'I've had a lot on'.

CRAIG: I've not been especially. I've not had a lot on.

MARTIN: I see. Fuck off Martin.

CRAIG: Don't you think it'd be best if you just went –

MARTIN: Do you?

CRAIG: Martin: stop writing the fucking script for me.

MARTIN: Where would they get another actor at such short notice?

CRAIG: (*Shrugging.*) Stay if you want. But do us all a favour and keep it down. (*Turns away.*)

MARTIN: About the other week.

CRAIG: (*Not looking up.*) Which has nothing to do with anything –

MARTIN: Look – I just wanted to say – I'm – well – sorry.

CRAIG: Okay. (*A pause.*)

MARTIN: For whatever it is I'm supposed to have done. (*A pause.*) For whatever it is that's making you treat me like something the dog shat out – If I *have* offended you in some way I'm very sorry – if not – well, give a guy a break– I'm nervous enough as it is –

CRAIG: So why do it?

MARTIN: If I do it – I get to sleep with you again. I know – is this man mad or what –

CRAIG: Look – what happened between us was –

MARTIN: Just sex, I know. You made that pretty damn clear.

CRAIG: I know.

MARTIN: Fuck 'em and forget 'em. But surely – just for today – I mean it'll make things a bit easier if we're okay with each other –

CRAIG: It doesn't make a scrap of difference. If we do shag on camera, believe me, it'll be lights on, camera on, shag, come, stop – end of story. That it, that's as far as it goes. Five minutes of business and finito.

MARTIN: I know you think I'm desperately love with you –

CRAIG: (*Indifferently.*) Aren't you?

MARTIN: No –

CRAIG: Good.

MARTIN: I've no problem. This boy's raring to go.

CRAIG: I don't feel anything –

MARTIN: I know –

CRAIG: (*Coming closer.*) Anything emotional that is –

MARTIN: I read you loud and clear. (*They kiss.*)

CRAIG: Since that night I've had sex four times. Four different men –

MARTIN: (*Breaking back, shocked at this.*) Okay –

CRAIG: No cards, no calls, no cups of tea, no walks in the bloody woods. Just sex. Four fucks. It's what I want.

MARTIN: Sure –

CRAIG: As long as you're clear about that.

MARTIN: Just tell me one thing –

CRAIG: What?

MARTIN: Tell me that the other week meant nothing to you –

CRAIG: The other week meant nothing to me – (*A pause.*) Look, don't you think you'd be happier if you went?

MARTIN: What the fuck do you know about what makes me happy? What do you even know about *happy*? (*A pause, he tries again.*) I thought we shared something –

CRAIG: I kissed you – on a count of three I stuck my tongue in – let my breath out. (*Deliberately cruel.*) On a count of five I ran my hands lightly down your side – ran them back up, and pulled off your top. I kissed you again and then ran my tongue down your neck to your left nipple. Tongue two three, then right nipple, tongue two three – as one hand started to pull down your fly –

MARTIN: You bastard –

CRAIG: Yes. If that makes you feel any better – yes, it's Mr Bastard appearing live in *Hot Shooting Boys 2*. (*More gently.*) Don't you think you should go?

MARTIN: Maybe I should. (*He's about to go – but at the door he turns.*) I've never met anyone like you – You don't even keep your books. Like you meet someone – go to bed with them – you get to know something about them. Their favourite colour or *something*. All I know is you're from Bridlington – and I found that out from someone else.

At that moment KEVIN comes in wearing his gear for the shoot.

KEVIN: What d'you think lads?

MARTIN: Very nice Kev –

KEVIN: These pants are killing me –

MARTIN: Never mind, it doesn't half show your arse off –

KEVIN: This heterosexual thanks you –

MARTIN: This homosexual says who are you trying to kid?

ROBERT enters wearing mechanics gear.

ROBERT: They said to say they'll be starting with the dreaded page seventy-two.

KEVIN: What page's that?

ROBERT: The scene with the three of us – there's something about the lights being needed by six for an Asian wedding party –

KEVIN: Martin, they said to say they'll be ready for you and Craig after we've done that.

CRAIG: Martin's not doing it –

KEVIN: I thought you were –

CRAIG: Well he's not –

MARTIN: Whatever gave you that idea?

CRAIG: Martin –

MARTIN: (*By now a bit drunk.*) I wouldn't miss this for the world. 'Sex to me – it's about energy – excitement' – something like that – As I said – this boy's raring to go.

CRAIG: Did they say how long?

ROBERT: Ten minutes tops –

CRAIG: (*Switching into life.*) Okay lads, maybe we'd better get ourselves ready. Perhaps a couple of breathing exercises – not you Martin – just us in the scene.

KEVIN: Right – I know this dead good one –

CRAIG: So do I – let's all just stand in a semi-circle – breathe in deeply – right in – and out – in and out – out – I want to feel your diaphragm moving up and down –

As he does so he goes to both ROBERT and KEVIN and feels their chests moving from behind. His voice becomes low and seductive.

Keep breathing – in, out – in out – try and get your body totally relaxed. That's right. Still and relaxed. Because soon we're going to go and we're going to enjoy ourselves. We're going to have a good time with each other. Nothing heavy, nothing deep – just sex. Nothing dirty, nothing unnatural – just us – giving each other pleasure – Okay? Kevin?

He kisses him. Nervously KEVIN responds.

That's not so good – let's try Robert.

He kisses him. ROBERT responds better.

That's more like it – let's try Kev again.

This time KEVIN responds. Upset, MARTIN exits.

Cut to: The lights coming on, talking, noise as the three prepare themselves, KEVIN does acting exercises, ROBERT hovers about unsure etc. They spray themselves with a plant sprayer to simulate sweat. They take up their position – and the noise switches to that of a raunchy porn music drumbeat.

CRAIG: So that's that sorted out –

KEVIN: Yes.

ROBERT: Sorted out except for one thing –

CRAIG: What's that then?

ROBERT: You still owe me –

CRAIG: I said – I'll pay when I can.

KEVIN: Talking of which you owe me as well –

CRAIG: I said – I've not got the money –

ROBERT: Who said anything about money?

KEVIN: Yeah –

ROBERT: Let's do him –

CRAIG: Yes please mister –

Crappy music soundtrack starts. (NB. When the strobe comes on we can hear what they're really thinking: the words they say aloud as part of the script are in bold italics.)

KEVIN: God –

CRAIG: Here we go –

ROBERT: We're off –

CRAIG: Amateur half-hour.

KEVIN: God, here we go –

ROBERT: ***We'll make you pay college boy.***

MARTIN: He strips Craig's shirt off.

CRAIG: Careful –

KEVIN: *Yeah – strip that fucker.*

MARTIN: He undoes Craig's trousers.

CRAIG: Get on with it then –

KEVIN: Icebergs – freezers – frosty days –

CRAIG: And pull the shorts down – slowly – slowly –

   They nearly topple over.

   You're pulling a boloody blind –

MARTIN: They free his cock.

CRAIG: Trembling hands or what –

ROBERT: That's some stiffy –

CRAIG: He obviously doesn't get it much –

KEVIN: My dog is dead, my dog is dead –

ROBERT: *You suck that dick college boy.*

CRAIG: My knee hurts like buggary –

KEVIN: Breathe – breathe.

CRAIG: *Yes please Mister* – shit –

ROBERT: I hope his mouth's clean.

CRAIG: He's gagging for it –

ROBERT: That's good head –

CRAIG: Dettol?

ROBERT: Don't stop – *Oh yes* –

CRAIG: *Mmmm.*

KEVIN: Breathe breathe breathe –

CRAIG: *Let's suck your dick now Mister –*

KEVIN: *Sure –*

ROBERT: Is he for real?

CRAIG: Straight my arse – (*He undoes his trousers.*)

ROBERT: Stiff as a bloody board –

CRAIG: Calm down for God's sake –

ROBERT: *Suck that cock.*

KEVIN: Find the feeling, find the feeling –

ROBERT: He must work out –

KEVIN: Bland Decker drills – Asda shopping – my dog is dead – (*His voice goes up.*)

CRAIG: Bloody amateurs –

ROBERT: *Go on then college boy – rim me –*

CRAIG: Oh fuck –

KEVIN: *Do it –*

CRAIG: I hate rimming –

ROBERT: *Oh yes –*

MARTIN: Robert bends over and parts his cheeks.

CRAIG: I hope he's wiped properly – *Go on Mister – let me give you some tongue –*

ROBERT: *Give me your tongue* – That's good –

CRAIG: Savlon?

ROBERT: Don't stop –

MARTIN: He rims him.

KEVIN: *Now, college boy, give me your tight arse.*

MARTIN: Without stopping he parts his cheeks.

ROBERT: Go on then – give it to him.

CRAIG: Talk about bloody Laurel and Hardy. ***Go on then Mister – give it me.*** Aahhh –

ROBERT: He's warm –

KEVIN: His hair –

ROBERT: He's so warm –

KEVIN: His hair smells of –

ROBERT: Hot –

KEVIN: Coconut oil –

ROBERT: There's a birthmark on his neck –

CRAIG: His aftershave –

KEVIN: Smudge of make up –

CRAIG: Vanilla –

ROBERT: His ribs are hot –

CRAIG: Sweet vanilla –

KEVIN: Terracotta on his colla –

ROBERT: His –

KEVIN: His –

CRAIG: Sweet –

KEVIN: Smudge –

ROBERT: Warm…

The three orgasm – and freeze in their position.

KEVIN: What the fuck have I done?

ROBERT: What am I doing here?

Abruptly the lights cut, and the three overbalance and fall, CRAIG landing on his knee.

KEVIN: What is it?

ROBERT: Power cut?

KEVIN: (*Upset.*) Fuck –

ROBERT: Must be all these lights – blown a fuse.

KEVIN: Fuck fuck fuck –

CRAIG: We just did – Of course we'll have to re-shoot.

ROBERT: Sorry?

CRAIG: Reshoot – do it again.

ROBERT: Because of the lights going out –

CRAIG: Because it was crap.

ROBERT: Sorry?

CRAIG: Crap. Shit, crap and bollocks – The rhythm was out of synch; the timing was just ridiculous and when you do suck someone's dick you should at least try not to be like a kid of fucking six with a fucking strawberry Mivvy.

There's a shocked silence. MARTIN enters with a torch.

MARTIN: (*A bit drunk – and oblivious.*) Knock knock. You all decent? Silly question Martin. (*He produces a metal candlesick in the shape of a Christmas tree.*) I got this – it's the best I could do – It's the main fuse – they said to say the circuit breakers kicked in – and knacked out – so obviously you were really going it some – (*There is no response to this.*) It's okay, one of your boys has got someone onto it – they'll be out here in a bit – they said all we have to do is sit tight and wait – (*MARTIN lights the candle. It looks very atmospheric.*) So – good scene? It looked pretty hot – quite got me in the mood myself –

CRAIG: The best.

MARTIN: Hey I – I don't believe it – lads – look outside –

ROBERT: What?

MARTIN: It's snowing –

CRAIG: Did they say how long?

MARTIN: Ah, shut up moaning – I found this. (*He choose a CD and presses play. A carol starts playing.*) Christmas time is officially here –

Despite themselves the men stand looking out at the snow, listening to the carol. Spotlight on ROBERT.

ROBERT: It's like feathers – dirty great fat feathers – starting to catch – making everything white – roofs – pavements – roads – The whole world gone white – (*He stands alone, spot-lit, remembering.*) The road outside the cathedral crammed with cars – making black ribbons in the snow – all the windows of all the houses in the Close lit up with fairy lights – the church starting to fill.

MR WALTON: Robert –

ROBERT: Hi Mr Walton –

MR WALTON: There you are – I've been looking for you all over –

ROBERT: I've been looking at the snow –

MR WALTON: Going to make a snowman?

ROBERT: (*As if he's being obviously childish.*) No –

MR WALTON: Come here –

ROBERT: What?

MR WALTON: Call that ruff straight? Can't have our lead man looking a scruff, can we? There, that's better. Hello.

ROBERT: Hello.

MR WALTON: Happy Christmas.

ROBERT: Happy Christmas.

MR WALTON: I got you something –

ROBERT: A gold chain. In a black velvet box. Real gold?

MR WALTON: Of course.

ROBERT: I hold it in my palm. Cold. It coils and slinks through my fingers.

MR WALTON: D'you want me to put it on for you?

ROBERT: Okay.

MR WALTON: There. God, you look lovely.

ROBERT: Thanks.

MR WALTON: I'll maybe see you after the service?

ROBERT: If you want –

MR WALTON: You can say thank you properly –

ROBERT: Yes –

MR WALTON: Usual place.

ROBERT: If the Dean comes I'll say I'm looking for my gloves.

MR WALTON: And if anyone asks – about the chain –

ROBERT: I'll say a friend got it for me –

MR WALTON: Good lad. Oh, and remember –

ROBERT: Yes?

MR WALTON: That first line – smooth – 'where a mother lay her baby…'

ROBERT: Yes Sir. (*MR WALTON fades back. The carol 'Once in Royal David's City' starts. Smiling, proud.*) Walking in at the head of the choir. Faces turned to me. Smiling. Teary. My family. Teachers from school. Mr Walton at the organ. 'He sings like an angel' someone says. And all the time the chain cold against my neck – (*He steps back.*)

Shakily KEVIN goes and looks out of the window.

KEVIN: (*As an adult.*) It's really thick now – across the road in one of the houses – someone's decorating a tree – tinsel – baubles – lights – And the lights go on and off – red and blue and yellow – on and off. (*As a child.*) Presents piled underneath – spilling out across the floor – and on the radio the Queen – a smell of coffee and turkey coming from the kitchen – and the presents –

FATHER: Steady on –

KEVIN: Please –

FATHER: Not till we've cleared the breakfast things –

KEVIN: Just one –

FATHER: You heard me.

KEVIN: Yes Dad. A hundred years later they're done – and I dive at the presents, the paper slippery under my fingers – tearing through robins and snowmen and Santas –

FATHER: Steady on, it's not a race –

KEVIN: A Meccano set – a *Beano* annual –

FATHER: Now then –

KEVIN: A cricket bat –

FATHER: That'll see you right –

MOTHER: Kevin –

KEVIN: Thanks Dad –

FATHER: We can go down the rec later – have a knock about –

MOTHER: That's a good idea –

KEVIN: And a box.

FATHER: What's that?

MOTHER: It's from our Marion –

FATHER: Her –

MOTHER: Keith.

KEVIN: A woman – looking into a mirror – her face all done up. (*Reads.*) Complete Stage Make Up Kit –

FATHER: You what?

KEVIN: Pictures of faces done up – a witch – a cat – a dragon –

FATHER: Make up?

MOTHER: Stage make up – she thought seeing as how he seemed interested, after he did so well in the show at church –

FATHER: Bloody hell –

MOTHER: Keith –

KEVIN: Greasepaint – and all little pots – labelled – freckle brown – blood red – dragon green.

FATHER: Your sister.

MOTHER: (*Weary.*) Come on Keith –

FATHER: I tell you, there's no son of mine going to be playing with make up – any sort of make up –

KEVIN: Dad!

FATHER: Give it here – you don't want that – I don't know what she was thinking of –

MOTHER: Keith, for God's sakes –

FATHER: Trust me – you don't want that –

KEVIN: He took it out into the back garden with all the wrapping paper. Tipped it all into the brazier. Got out the matches. I could see the lady's face begin to blacken. Curl. The smoke was all funny. Later on I went and had a look. The pots were all black. Greasy looking. Freckle brown. Blood red. Dragon green.

CRAIG sits alone. MARTIN enters with thermos.

CRAIG: Before you ask I am absolutely fucking fine.

MARTIN: Always are, aren't you. I just wondered if you wanted a brew – (*CRAIG says nothing. MARTIN pours some coffee.*)

CRAIG: Thanks.

MARTIN: It's turning to slush. I reckon it'll be gone in an hour. Here. (*CRAIG turns to get the coffee and winces.*) Come on – yeah I know, it's fine – so it won't hurt you to let me have a look. Don't worry, it's only your knee I'm after. For now –

CRAIG: I know what it is –

MARTIN: So you know where it'll hurt –

CRAIG: Owww –

MARTIN: Give it up – there we are –

CRAIG: You've done this before –

MARTIN: I used to work in an old folks' home remember– (*CRAIG winces.*) It's the cartilage.

CRAIG: I know it's the fucking cartilage.

MARTIN: So you'll know it should be supported. (*Expertly he manipulates the knee.*)

CRAIG: Yes.

MARTIN: Do Calvin Klein do support bandages we ask ourselves? Sorry – look –I just wanted to say – About later – you and me –

CRAIG: What about it?

MARTIN: I just wanted to say – Don't worry. I'm making a compartment in my head. (*He finishes with the knee.*) It's like you said – just a shag. I'll be fine –

CRAIG: Look Martin. (*He stops.*) Thanks for the coffee.

MARTIN exits, leaving CRAIG alone. He stands and as he does the sound of the sea fades up. Faintly in the background is a party with Christmas music playing. He sits, rubs his knee in pain. One of the men enters as GRAHAM, from the past.

GRAHAM: Craig – hold on mate – what are you doing – are you okay?

CRAIG: I just slipped on the ice.

GRAHAM: I'm not surprised – you were running like the bloody six million-dollar man. What's up?

CRAIG: Nothing –

GRAHAM: I know the disco's bad but this is ridiculous.

CRAIG: You should be back in there –

GRAHAM: I'm all right for five minutes –

CRAIG: Man of the moment –

GRAHAM: Are you sure you're okay?

CRAIG: If you must know I was going to hewwy –

GRAHAM: Shite man – you okay now?

CRAIG: Yeah – I reckon the cold must've cleared my head.

GRAHAM: It's bloody freezing. They reckon snow's forecast – (*A pause.*) Hey – remember that time we tipped snow down Clare Hewitt's neck? I got sent to Mr Sloan, you had to stand by the wall –

CRAIG: And now you're getting engaged –

GRAHAM: Yeah –

CRAIG: It's a good turn out –

GRAHAM: There would be –

CRAIG: Natalie looks happy.

GRAHAM: She is –

CRAIG: You're a lucky man –

GRAHAM: So everyone keeps telling me.

CRAIG: I hope you'll be very happy.

GRAHAM: Shut the fuck up and let's have a look at that knee –

CRAIG: It's nothing –

GRAHAM: Shut up – here – does that hurt?

CRAIG: Of course it does you arsehole. Look, it's nothing, I just twisted it. (*Slow Christmas music starts in the background.*) It's the slow dance –

GRAHAM: Is it?

CRAIG: You'd better get back.

GRAHAM: Yeah –

CRAIG: They'll want you to start the dancing –

GRAHAM: Yeah. (*Suddenly, clumsily he kisses CRAIG – it's more of a bumping of faces. CRAIG pulls back.*)

CRAIG: Fuck off –

GRAHAM: Sorry –

CRAIG: What's your problem?

GRAHAM: Sorry – I must be pissed –

CRAIG: It's okay.

GRAHAM: Look – I'm really sorry –

CRAIG: I said – it's okay –

GRAHAM: I better get back then.

CRAIG: Yeah.

GRAHAM fades into the background. CRAIG stands on his own. Noise around him – business. Lights being set up, sound levels being tested, as before. Someone shouts action. CRAIG stays where he is. We hear the following.

MARTIN: Hey – (*CRAIG looks up vaguely.*) Sorry mate, didn't mean to scare you. (*CRAIG doesn't respond. MARTIN gamely ploughs on.*) I'm the electrician. I heard there's a plug gone. (*He looks at CRAIG.*) Where is it? The plug? (*Still CRAIG isn't responding.*) I'll just have a look shall I –

Standing facing CRAIG, MARTIN gets his dick out (back to the audience). CRAIG stands –

CRAIG: I'm sorry –

MARTIN: What?

CRAIG: Sorry –

He runs off, leaving MARTIN looking after him.

MARTIN: Shit –

Cut to: CRAIG on his own, getting dressed. Rosemary Clooney plays. MARTIN enters, stands looking at him.

MARTIN: What? *What?*

CRAIG: Can we just leave it –

MARTIN: They said you'd lost your bottle, I said not you. Anyone but you. I mean you are Mr Fuck 'Em and Forget 'Em.

CRAIG: They're right.

MARTIN: What?

CRAIG: I have. Lost my bottle.

MARTIN: It's me isn't it?

CRAIG: No.

MARTIN: I mean okay, you might as well say it – I know I'm not the world's best –

CRAIG: I said it's not you.

MARTIN: I am I that crap?

CRAIG: No –

MARTIN: So what? Just what is it? I mean come on, you're the bloody one bloody well going on about bloody compartments in the head – so where's the fucking problem? You shag me, end of story. I go and see Guy; you go and grope whoever it is down the Mineshaft or wherever, end of story. No problem. Come on. I'm up for it. If it's not a problem for me you should be fine, old hand like yourself. Just two people having a shag.

CRAIG: Come away with me –

MARTIN: (*This is the last thing he'd expected.*) What?

CRAIG: Away – from here – from this place – we don't want to be doing this. (*MARTIN takes CRAIG's hand – but CRAIG withdraws it.*) No, Martin, that's not what I mean.

MARTIN: I don't understand you.

CRAIG: I know – (*He turns to go.*)

MARTIN: You're fucked up, you know that?

CRAIG: Yes I do –

MARTIN: Go on then –

CRAIG: Martin –

MARTIN: Piss off if you're going. (*CRAIG goes to exit. At the door he turns.*)

CRAIG: It's red.

MARTIN: What?

CRAIG: My favourite colour. (*Exits.*)

Music fades up – the crappy jazzy porn film soundtrack. We see KEVIN and ROBERT stood watching, faces expressionless. We hear a snatch of dialogue from the film – the scene CRAIG, KEVIN and ROBERT were making:

CRAIG: I said – I'll pay when I can.

KEVIN: Talking of which you owe me as well –

CRAIG: I said – I've not got the money –

ROBERT: Who said anything about money?

KEVIN: Yeah –

ROBERT: Let's do him –

CRAIG: Yes please mister –

Crappy music soundtrack starts plus a series of grunts. They fade and the lights come up. They become aware of each other.

ROBERT: So this is what they call a 'screening' –

KEVIN: When I did stuff with the Beeb we used Soho House –

ROBERT: Hardly the most salubrious of places – I just hope my car's all right outside – (*They sip their wine and pull a face.*) So, on your own are you?

KEVIN: It's Jess's Pilates night – you?

ROBERT: Marcus's working late. Anyway he's already seen it.

KEVIN: Oh?

ROBERT: He was very sweet. 'Robert', he said – 'A star is porn'. Bought me a magnum of my favourite champagne –

KEVIN: Can't be bad.

ROBERT: And Jess?

KEVIN: What?

ROBERT: What did she make of it?

KEVIN: You know – just another job. (*They react to a request for photos.*) Okay –

ROBERT: Sure – both together?

KEVIN: Like this? (*They pose together.*)

ROBERT: (*As they pose.*) They asked me to do another you know –

KEVIN: Did they?

ROBERT: *Hot Shooting Boys 3* –

KEVIN: Are you going to?

ROBERT: Well, it's when we're going to Tuscany –

KEVIN: Right.

ROBERT: Oh – and I'm taking up paragliding. (*Flashes go off.*)

KEVIN: Oh?

ROBERT: Place near Dorking – very reasonable – well it isn't but what the hell. So what about you?

KEVIN: What?

ROBERT: The acting. Kickstarting the old career –

KEVIN: Yes, good. Lots of interest.

ROBERT: Oh?

KEVIN: Nothing definite – but then there never is – until there is. But we're getting married –

ROBERT: You and Jess?

KEVIN: Yes. twenty-fifth of next month.

ROBERT: (*Amused.*) Congratulations –

KEVIN: (*The photos stop.*) That okay? (*They stand apart slightly awkward now the photographers have gone.*) So – how did you get here?

ROBERT: North circular –

KEVIN: What's that like at this time of night?

ROBERT: Fucking joke –

KEVIN: Oh?

ROBERT: One-way system near Kentish town – I mean I ask you –

KEVIN: I know this cut-through –

ROBERT: – by Regents Park –

KEVIN: Speed bump city but much quicker.

Enter MARTIN, slightly the worse for drink.

MARTIN: It's my beloved co-stars – (*In response to request for photos.*) The three of us – sure – so what did you think?

ROBERT: It was okay –

MARTIN: I tell you something – you two looked pretty damn horny – I tell you something Kev, you can't half shift that arse when you get going – loads of people were saying so – That bit where you stuck those jump leads up his bum – Hey – You see him over there? Old git – tongue down to his knees? He loved it – said I had a real sexual presence – I thought, 'Hello, your eyes must be even worse than they look' – still, owns a house in Holland Park thank you very much so can't be bad – oh, and between you and me – and this must go absolutely no further – there's even talk of a Stiffy in the air – Even without the presence of our beloved co-star – though speaking personally I can't say he was greatly missed –

ROBERT: No –

MARTIN: That Hungarian thing they got for me did very nicely thank you very much.

KEVIN: Right –

MARTIN: Don't suppose anyone's seen anything of him? Old Jude Law?

KEVIN: No – listen –

ROBERT: Gone back home I think –

MARTIN: What?

ROBERT: That's what someone was saying –

MARTIN: Well as far as I'm concerned Skegness is welcome to him – Quite common in this business apparently – the old burn out – you've either got it or you haven't – Just me? Yes, sure –

He steps forward alone. The other two fade into the background. Unabashed he cradles his drink lost in thought. The lights dim until he's in a spot.

A real sexual presence – Martin, you have a real sexual presence –

The noise of the sea comes up.

Since the film there's been no looking back for this boy. Overload have signed me up for another three – stack of photo shoots, some solo, some with some very interesting guys with the most enormous willies you ever did see… *And* – and this is massively exciting – there's even talk of me maybe trying my hand in LA as it were – apparently the Brits are very big in the old porn business out there – something to do with sounding classy when you come. (*The sound of the sea.*) Now that'd be something – Los bloody Angeles –

Lights up on CRAIG.

CRAIG: I'm walking down the beach.

MARTIN: This guy is on his way –

CRAIG: Feet slithering in the shingle.

MARTIN: And if the old U S of A does work out – there's loads of men out there, all totally loaded.

CRAIG: In the distance I can see the Spurn point light – far away –

MARTIN: Just waiting to fall in love with me –

CRAIG: Once every thirty seconds – flash flash –

MARTIN: Gym fit, beach houses – a swimming pool –

CRAIG: Bright in the distance –

MARTIN: (*Softly.*) Martin: you have a real sexual presence –

CRAIG: Nothing but the wind and the sea and the distant light –

The light fades on him – then abruptly fades up with the porn track – a snatch of dialogue which jams and repeats – and is replaced by static.

The End.